THE
MIGHTY EIGHTH
IN ART

THE MIGHTY EIGHTH
IN ART

ROGER A. FREEMAN

ARMS AND
ARMOUR

ARMS & ARMOUR PRESS
An imprint of the Cassell Group
Wellington House, 125 Strand, London WC2R 0BB

Distributed in the USA by Sterling Publishing Co. Inc., 387 Park
Avenue South, New York, NY 10016-8810

Distributed in Australia by Capricorn Link (Australia) Pty Ltd, 2/13
Carrington Road, Castle Hill, New South Wales 2154

British Library Cataloguing-in-Publication data:
A catalogue record for this book is available from the British Library.

ISBN 1 85409 312 6

Edited and designed by Roger Chesneau/DAG Publications Ltd

Printed and bound in Slovenia by printing house Gorenjski tisk
by arrangement with Korotan, Ljubljana.

Contents

Introduction

THE word 'art' embraces a varied range of work resulting from human skills. However, in general parlance, art implies pictorial creations. Before the introduction of the camera the painter served as much to make a visual record as to offer something pleasing to the viewer. People, places and events of earlier years were presented to us by the contemporary painters, albeit that even then, to appease their patrons, enhancing embellishments were common. Human conflicts, on sea and land, have always been popular subjects, and while the commissioning of artists to accompany armies and navies into battle is not a recent innovation, for the most part the paintings of such events were the result of the painters' imagination from the safety of their studios. Further to gain approval of the artists' work, the carnage on the battlefield or warship deck was muted if not sanitised.

The advent of photography caused the artist to adopt a more realistic approach. Starker images are found in the war art of the late nineteenth and early twentieth century. Even so, the painter, mindful that few if any patrons would wish to adorn their walls with scenes of horror, wisely chose to avoid the results of extreme violence upon the human form lest the sales of his work be harmed and subject to censure. Modern naval engagements offered opportunities that would not offend the sensibilities of customers because the humans involved could be hidden by the structures of the vessel. Equally fulfilling were military aircraft for, like warships, the men within being mostly concealed from view, it was machines that became the combatants,

allowing far more antagonistic scenes to be devised. Air battles with twisting, diving and falling aircraft became an attractive subject for war artists during and after the 1914–18 conflict. But air actions and aircraft in general did not become truly popular for portrayal as art until the latter part of the twentieth century. The reasons are primarily the public's greater exposure to aviation and subsequent interest, combined with the availability of prints at prices within the reach of the pockets of most.

The art world is well know for its élitism, and at one time he or she who featured a machine in a drawing or painting was inclined to be seen as a technical illustrator. Aeroplanes were definitely not popular subjects for 'real' art during the first half of this century. While they may still be condemned by some doyens who would not consider even the best as fine art, there has been a general mellowing of attitudes, no doubt occasioned by the number of leading artists who now apply their talents to aviation scenes.

Aircraft subjects allow a considerable diversity in backgrounds and a wide scope for artistic interpretation. However, the aeroplane itself is subject to strict criteria, again arising from the censures of photography. The different makes and models of aircraft, each with their specific shapes, have been so well portrayed in photographs as to exact a discipline upon the artist: his representation must take no liberties with form or detail, for the dedicated collector of art originals or prints expects the aeroplane to be true to its real image in form and colour—

no artist's licence here: the proportions and curves must be nearly exact, and even the detail markings must show resemblance to reality. The collector of aviation art has come to expect this reality and will reject that which is inaccurate or veers towards impressionism.

Interestingly, the contemporary Second World War artists' work did not suffer these strictures: an impression was acceptable in most circles. The aeroplanes of quite distinguished artists in the United Kingdom and the United States would in some cases not pass as truly accurate renderings of the types portrayed, and they probably owed their popularity and acclaim to the Expressionist cult, the twentieth century movement which favoured a direct expression of the artist's feeling as against other considerations.

While aviation art now strongly fosters realism, bringing it for visual impact in close competition with large colour photographic prints, there is one area where the artist is in a far superior position. Pleasing photographs of aeroplanes are commonplace, but photographs of air combat are few, often indistinct and of restricted view. Aerial combat at high speeds was a series of fleeting happenings. The artist can not only capture such moments in his work, but he can present them in a panorama beyond the compass of the cameras of the day.

The United States Eighth Air Force of the Second World War has attracted many artists. While the historic aspects of this, the largest air striking force of that conflict, are enticing, so too is the unusually colourful decor of its aircraft, particularly during the closing months of hostilities. The bright colours stemmed from the need for the quick and positive identification of units in the air, and with some 200 such units the range of these colour markings was considerable. For many artists the choice of subject appears to be motivated by a desire to combine an historic incident with a good colour range and, for the reasons just explored, to have a good reference to aid accuracy. As might be expected, the same or similar subjects have been portrayed

by several artists: in one case at least ten commercial enterprises have painted the same or an allied incident with a view to producing prints. Famous units such as the 4th and 56th Fighter Groups and the 91st and 100th Bomb Groups are also in preponderance. Apart from artists like Keith Hill, who was commissioned by the Eighth Air Force Memorial Museum Foundation (a veterans' organisation) to make a painting representative of every flying group in the Eighth Air Force, most artists favour the better-known units, with the result that there are many others that have been sadly neglected among the hundreds of paintings considered for this volume.

It should be made clear that the compiler has not sat as judge or critic: the aim has been to present a variety of approaches, from a reasonably large number of artists. As will be seen, this includes those who are acclaimed as being at the top of their profession and a few who might honestly be described as newcomers. The criteria for selection also included subjects that were spread throughout the 1942–45 period of Eighth Air Force operations, and coverage of as many different units as the presentations allowed. There may well be those who do not hold with some of the works selected or regret that other works are not to be seen in the following pages. To provide something palatable for all tastes, a deliberate effort has been made to achieve as much variety with types and styles as possible. The order in which the paintings are presented is broadly chronological. Where generic subjects were involved the factors deciding their place in the sequence have been the decor and model of the aircraft and the background season.

The official fostering of American artists, to portray the Eighth Air Force during its early days in Britain, was limited to a visit by Peter Hurd in 1942 and Tom Lea while passing through a year later. Surprisingly, the most prolific painter of Eighth Air Force subjects was a British artist, Frank E. Beresford, who was given official US war correspondent status to aid and encourage his work. He produced the largest collection of contemporary paintings depicting personnel and activities, of which most canvases are now in USAF ownership.

The Eighth Air Force had many men who were professional artists in civilian life and others who were extremely talented amateurs. Understandably, it was the British countryside and cities that they most wished to record on card, canvas or paper; comparatively few chose, or were officially encouraged, to use their talents to record the war in which they were involved. Their activities with brush and paints were chiefly evident in the murals to be found at almost every airfield station, or as motifs or pictorial embellishments upon the warplanes they flew or supported. In recent years the latter, which after the war came to be known as 'nose art', has gathered something of a cult following, such was the craft, humour and ingenuity of this work. Being on what was to all intents and purposes an expendable machine, the result of many hours of skilled application was frequently destroyed within days. The murals were more durable, and a few have been preserved.

The artist's eye could not and cannot match the camera lens for truth, but it provides something of far greater value. Combining knowledge and imagination, the artist can produce an evocation; he or she can present us with a permanent impression of a happening gone in a fraction of a second which even the combatants involved could not see completely. As can be seen in this volume, many of these evocations are spell-binding. Yet some connoisseurs of art may still find them alien. Beauty is, as always, in the eye of the beholder.

ACKNOWLEDGEMENTS

The compiler wishes to thank all contributing artists for permission to include their work. In addition, he gratefully acknowledges the assistance of the following persons and establishments for providing information and material for this publication: John Blake of the Guild of Aviation Artists, Keith Braybrook, William S. Deakyne, Christine Gregory of the Royal Air Force Museum, Patrica Keen, Walter Konantz, Allen Ostrom, Geoff Ward, Joan Celeste Thomas of the US Army Center of Military History, the USAF Art Program, the staff of the Imperial War Museum Art Collection and, on the production side, Bruce Robertson for editorial guidance, Ian Mactaggart for photography, and Jean Freeman and Alison Apricot for the preparation of the text.

ROGER A. FREEMAN

'First Mission'

NIXON GALLOWAY

THE initial offensive air operation conducted by the United States Army Air Forces in the European Theatre of Operations was staged on 4 July 1942. More than an element of flag-waving was involved in the selection of American Independence Day to launch the first bombing raid. Chiefly for home morale reasons, the politicians and senior military commanders in the United States were impatient for early action from the air forces being sent to the United Kingdom.

The only unit in place by mid-summer was a light bomber squadron being tutored by the Royal Air Force in its methods of attack. It was this, the 15th Bomb Squadron (L), that was alerted to enter the fray, although it had no aircraft of its own and would have to borrow Douglas Bostons from its RAF mentor, No 226 Squadron. A joint operation was planned with a dozen Bostons, six of which would be manned by crews of the 15th Bomb Squadron. Targets selected were four Luftwaffe airfields in occupied Holland, each to be attacked at very low level by a flight of three aircraft. The flights with US participants were all to be led by experienced RAF crews.

Unfortunately, in the event, the enemy's defences received an early alert, probably from coastal vessels on patrol. Three Bostons, two American crewed and one British, failed to return. Concentrated ground fire at two airfields accounted for two of the bombers and the third was apparently shot down by an enemy fighter. It was hardly a successful operation as only limited damage was done to the airfields attacked. Fortunate to return was the aircraft flown by 15th Bomb Squadron's CO, Captain Charles Kegelman. Swooping across De Kooy airfield, the Boston took a hit in the starboard engine, which lost its propeller. At the time Kegelman was just skimming the surface of the airfield and in a momentary loss of control the starboard wing-tip and the underside of the rear fuselage scraped the ground. Only Kegelman's superior piloting averted a crash, for he was able to right the Boston and climb away over the airfield boundary. A fire in the damaged engine disappeared, and after jettisoning the bomb load Kegelman brought the Boston back for a safe landing at Swanton Morley, the airfield from which the mission had been dispatched.

Nixon Galloway's thrilling recreation of a moment following Kegelman's impact with the enemy airfield shows a tongue of flame from the damaged engine as 'Z-Zebra' evades catastrophe and gains altitude. In the background the bombs from the flight leader explode among airfield buildings and the third member of the De Kooy flight is about to bomb.

'The Return from the Raid over Rouen'

PETER HURD

PETER Hurd's reputation as one of America's popular artists was established before the Second World War, most notably through his brilliant murals. Early in 1942 he was invited to become an officially approved war artist covering the USAAF, a selection of his work to be published in *Life* magazine. In April the 39-year-old artist flew to the United Kingdom and when the first heavy bomber group, the 97th, arrived with its B-17 Fortresses he moved to their station at Grafton Underwood. Here he was billeted with an officer of the 414th Bomb Squadron and spent the next few weeks sketching and painting the squadron's personnel, both around the base and while flying with them in their B-17Es on training missions. He stayed with the 97th until it moved to North Africa in November and shortly afterwards he returned to the United States.

Of his many paintings while in England, the best known is 'The Return from the Raid over Rouen'. Peter Hurd was present on 17 August 1942 when the Eighth Air Force's first heavy bomber mission was flown, and from sketches made while on the control tower he produced this painting in egg tempera. The leading flight of three B-17Es sweeps low in front of the control tower on return from bombing the railyards near the French town, while other aircraft involved circle the airfield. Group personnel and visitors have gathered to watch the homecoming and are delighted that all the bombers have returned. Parked near the artist's vantage point is a visiting RAF Spitfire and the Douglas C-47 transport that brought the official party from Eighth Air Force Headquarters. Vehicles seen include ambulances and fuel bowsers borrowed from the RAF in lieu of American equipment.

The original painting, together with most of Peter Hurd's wartime work, is hung in the US Army Art Collection in Washington, DC.

'1st Lt Carl E. Schultz'

PETER HURD

DURING Peter Hurd's stay with the 97th Bomb Group at Grafton Underwood in the summer and autumn of 1942, he produced a number of portraits of both air and ground personnel. Some of these paintings were derived from sketches made while flying with crews on training missions.

On one occasion he flew with Lieutenant Dowswell and his men in *Yankee Doodle*; sitting in the nose compartment, he drew bombardier Lieutenant Carl Schultz. The absence of oxygen mask and earphones over a service cap indicates flight at medium altitude. This was probably a gunnery mission as a .30-calibre machine gun is positioned in the right nosepiece socket. Schultz flew in the nose of *Yankee Doodle* on the Eighth Air Force's first heavy bomber mission, 17 August 1942, and survived his tour of duty in England to return to the United States in 1943.

Hurd's experience with the 97th had a profound effect on him. He was later to write to a friend: 'All in all, it was the biggest adventure I have ever had—living the life of constant excitement that is the life on a bomber station. They have the look of veterans, these youngsters in their late teens and early twenties. United in their supreme purpose, they have looked death in the face repeatedly and unflinchingly. They are invariably realists and know well the odds for and against their survival. But there is in them a will to endure—to endure beyond this struggle, if not as living men of flesh and blood, then in literature or in painting. So I had no lack of models. One thing was quickly apparent as I grew to know them well. There is no norm for a flier. They are of many types and classes and seem to have in common only courage, a love for flying and above all a belief in America's future as a free nation.'

'Yanks'

RONALD WONG

A PAIR of Spitfires meet the dawn over southern England. They display the red-outlined United States national insignia in use during the summer of 1943 and the unit identification letters 'ZM' of the 12th Reconnaissance Squadron then based at Membury, Wiltshire. The squadron was one of the oldest in the US service, having existed since 1917. It arrived in England in September 1942 as a unit of the 67th Observation Group, an organisation which became the sole USAAF practitioner of tactical reconnaissance in the United Kingdom. As the Eighth Air Force had no immediate operational requirement for supporting ground forces, the 67th perfected the art while also serving as a training and general duty organisation for a variety of duties and other commands.

The 67th Group's hedge-hopping Spitfire Vs were a familiar sight in southern counties during 1943. Some pilots were given operational experience through accompanying RAF fighter squadrons on cross-Channel combat sweeps. On one of these a 12th Reconnaissance Squadron pilot was shot down—the unit's first combat loss. In October 1943 the 67th Group and its squadrons were transferred to the US 9th Air Force, which was re-formed in the United Kingdom as the United States' element of the tactical air support for the invasion of continental Europe scheduled for the following spring. In the winter of 1943–44 the 12th Reconnaissance Squadron replaced its Spitfires with Mustangs.

Ronald Wong is a member of both Britain's Guild of Aviation Artists and the United States' equivalent, the American Society of Aviation Artists; the majority of his work features US subjects. He was born in China and spent most of his early years in Hong Kong. His art, which has won many awards and covers a wide spectrum of aviation, past and present, is usually created in acrylics.

'Shadow Companion'

FRANK WOOTTON OBE

ALONE, battle-damaged Fortress returns to England, its shadow thrown on the evening cumulus turned apricot by the sinking sun. Frank Wootton's representations of the airman's view of the elements is famous and his distinctive style sets him apart from other aviation artists. While the painting is not based on a specific incident and could be said to be generic, the subject aircraft bears the markings of the famous *Memphis Belle*. In fact, this 91st Bomb Group B-17F did, on 26 March 1943, sustain heavy damage to the fin and rudder similar that portrayed in 'Shadow Companion'.

Frank Wootton is an exhibitor at the Royal Academy, and in addition to aviation his fields are landscapes and equestrian studies. He has been the Honorary President of the Guild of Aviation Artists for more than two decades.

'Buckeye-Don'

HOWARD GERRARD

CLIPPED-WING Spitfire VBs shown against a wild undercast make up one of a series of paintings featuring the 4th Fighter Group which Howard Gerrard was inspired to create through his fascination with this famous fighter organisation.

The title, 'Buckeye-Don', refers to the slogan on the aircraft in the foreground which was assigned to Lieutenant Donald S. Gentile of the 336th Fighter Squadron from mid-October 1942 for six months. The original pilot complement of this and the other two squadrons of the 4th Fighter Group were American volunteers who had been formed into the so-called RAF Eagle Squadrons prior to the United States' becoming involved in hostilities. The RAF transferred the squadrons—together with their Spitfires and their Debden, Essex, base—to the Eighth Air Force in September 1942.

Don Gentile, a first-generation American of Italian immigrant parents, was an enthusiastic and able pilot who became one of the Eighth's outstanding fighter aces. His first combat sortie was flown in June 1942 and on 19 August that year he was credited with destroying two enemy aircraft during patrols in support of the Dieppe landings.

The 4th Group later converted to the P-47 Thunderbolt and then the P-51 Mustang, and it was with the latter type that Gentile starred, destroying ten enemy aircraft in air combat in March 1944 alone. The following month he was fêted as the leading US fighter pilot in Europe with 23 enemy aircraft destroyed in the air and seven on their airfields by strafing, a total that was later reduced by official reassessment.

Returning to the United Sates later that month, Gentile spent the remainder of the war on test-pilot duties. Tragically, as happened with several other distinguished pilots who survived hostilities, Don Gentile was killed in a post-war flying accident.

Spitfire *Buckeye-Don*, which Gentile last flew on 1 April 1943, had a motif comprising an eagle with boxing gloves painted on the fuselage below and forward of the cockpit. This was adopted by the 4th Fighter Group as its unofficial insignia.

'The Circus Outbound'

KEITH FERRIS

DURING the Second World War the United States' aircraft industry built more Consolidated B-24 Liberators than any other combat type. Liberators were used in a wide variety of roles, making a considerable contribution to the Allied cause. The aircraft's main employment was as a high-altitude heavy bomber, and although it performed with distinction it was not as well suited to the task as its running mate the B-17 Fortress. The operational technique of Eighth Air Force missions was based around flight at an optimum 25,000 feet, but fully loaded the B-24 was not stable at this altitude. Flying close-formation required hard work at the controls by the pilots and for this reason the Liberator was considered to be 'a man's aircraft'.

Owing to the demands of other services, the Eighth Air Force initially received only two groups of Liberators and one of those was not at full strength. This led to the B-24s' being used to meet contingencies elsewhere. The first Liberators to reach the Eighth Air Force were those of the 93rd Bomb Group in September 1942. Soon after the Group's operational début its squadrons were diverted to ocean patrols, a bad-weather project and a detachment to North Africa. As a result of this the 93rd dubbed itself 'Ted's Traveling Circus', 'Ted' being the CO, Colonel 'Ted' Timberlake.

Reunited, the 93rd flew its first bombing mission into Germany on 18 March 1943 against the submarine yards at Vegesack—a tough introduction as the formation encountered repeated interceptions most of the time it was over hostile territory. One B-24 was shot down and a few damaged against claims of five enemy fighters destroyed and several probables.

The 93rd's formation is seen leaving the coast of England for this mission in Keith Ferris's painting, with two famous Liberators of the 328th Bomb Squadron in the foreground both being original combat aircraft of the group. *Bomerang* eventually became the first B-24 in the Eighth Air Force to complete 50 missions and was retired to the United States in April 1944. *Shoot Luke* was not so fortunate: it was shot up during the 18 March mission depicted (as it was, indeed, on many other occasions) and was lost to enemy fighter attack seven months later.

The B-24 is an aircraft well known to the artist, for in 1943 his father commanded the B-24 transition school at Fort Worth, Texas. Keith was fourteen years old at the time and spent many hours watching the base's seventy Liberators come and go.

'A New Cyclone for Yankee Doodle'

JOHN YOUNG

BOVINGDON airfield in Hertfordshire was built as a bomber base in 1941 and from August 1942 was used by the Eighth Air Force as a Combat Crew Replacement Center. The purpose of this organisation was to indoctrinate new arrivals from the United States in the flying control and operating procedures used in the European theatre of war. Both ground school and airborne practice were involved, and for the latter B-17Es were employed. This model Fortress was brought to England by the first bomber group to arrive, the 97th, and, lacking many combat refinements, was a few weeks later turned over to the 92nd Bomb Group in exchange for its new B-17Fs. The 92nd was then given the task of manning and conducting the Combat Crew Replacement Center.

As a youngster John Young lived in the vicinity of Bovingdon and spent many out-of-school hours watching the B-17s come and go—little wonder, then, that favourite subjects for this distinguished aviation artist are the B-17Es of his teenage days. 'A New Cyclone for Yankee Doodle' depicts mechanics preparing a Wright R-1820 Cyclone radial for removal from B-17E number 19023, alias *Yankee Doodle*. A replacement engine hangs on the trolley hoist ready to become the bomber's new Number Three.

Yankee Doodle was of some fame, for, with its regular 414th Bomb Squadron crew, that of Lieutenant John P. Dowswell, it carried VIII Bomber Command's Brigadier General Ira Eaker on the Eighth Air Force's first heavy bomber raid, on 17 August 1942. After service at Bovingdon the aircraft was given to the 91st Bomb Group at Bassingbourn and for the remainder of the war was used by that organisation as a general hack for non-operational flights.

'Homeward Bound From St Nazaire'

KEITH HILL

THIS painting is one of a series of pictures featuring the actions which brought the award of the United States' highest decoration for bravery. 'Homeward Bound from St Nazaire' shows the 306th Bomb Group B-17F in which a deed of 'conspicuous gallantry and intrepidity' was performed on May Day 1943.

The target was the St Nazaire U-boat facilities, where cloud frustrated bombing and navigation. Disorientated, the 306th Bomb Group crossed what was assumed to be the coast of south-west England and began reducing altitude. They were met by a barrage of ground fire which brought down three of the bombers as they desperately tried to evade: it was not Land's End but the Brest peninsula. No sooner was the formation out of ground-fire range than enemy fighters attacked. The lowest, rearmost Fortress, 'V-Victor' of the 423rd Bomb Squadron, was raked from nose to tail with cannon shells and bullets. Three men were wounded and fires started in the radio room and near the tailwheel stowage. The radio man and two waist gunners, thinking the aircraft doomed, baled out over the sea.

Pilot 1st Lieutenant Lewis Johnson of 'V-Victor' was on the 25th and last mission of his tour. His ball-turret gunner, Sergeant Maynard Smith, was on his first. After the Fortress was hit 'Snuffy' Smith found the electrical controls of his turret inoperative so he climbed up into the fuselage. Despite seeing colleagues baling out, Smith set about fighting the fires with extinguishers and throwing out burning debris through a gaping hole in the right side of the radio room. When the extinguishers were exhausted, he emptied a water bottle over the flames and in exasperation urinated on the final smouldering embers. The heat had been so great that metal had melted and the integrity of the fuselage had been seriously weakened.

In between fighting the fires, Smith had attended to the badly wounded tail gunner and fired the occasional few rounds at enemy fighters from the waist guns. His actions had undoubtedly kept the bomber in the air and allowed Lewis Johnson to make an emergency landing at Predannack, Cornwall.

The Fortress was so badly damaged and weakened that it was beyond economical repair. Maynard Smith received the second Medal of Honor awarded an Eighth Air Force airman, the first to a surviving individual.

'Coming Home/England 1943'

GIL COHEN

THERE were at least three Fortresses in the Eighth Air Force named *Kayo* and two named *Katy*, and although this composition is generic it has the look of the 384th Bomb Group at Grafton Underwood which had a *Kayo* decorated in this style. Gil Cohen says: 'I wanted to name the B-17 in the picture after my granddaughter, Caitlin, but I wanted a great adjective before the name. A friend suggested a little belligerency—"K.O.", for knock-out, as in boxing: hence *Kayo Katy.*'

The crew major having his cigarette lit must be the Group's mission leader, for he has other senior officers and a Jeep to meet him. There is something reminiscent of Gregory Peck's Frank Savage in the epic movie *Twelve o'Clock High* about this character. The rest of the crew, no doubt about to board a '6 × 6' truck, carry A-3 equipment bags or chest pack parachutes and have the typical bomber crewman's garb of the period, most noticeably sheepskin flying jackets (worn examples of these were issued to ground crew members to lessen the chill of an English winter). One such recipient points to a battle-damage perforation in the cowling of No 2 engine; apparently the engine was little harmed as the propeller is not feathered. Finally, the cloud-filled sky and puddled hardstanding suggest a damp afternoon in late autumn. But the airmen are not worried about the weather: their faces confirm that the mission is over and they are home!

This painting was adjudged 'Best In Show' at the 1990 exhibition of the American Society of Aviation Artists.

'Return of the Belle'

ROBERT TAYLOR

BY whatever means, fame stems from publicity. The most famous of all Flying Fortress aircraft is that named *Memphis Belle*—whose fame is born of a film director's choice. To justify the investment in lives and material to the American public and explain the objectives, the Chief of the US Army Air Forces dispatched former Hollywood film director William Wyler to the United Kingdom with a brief to make a documentary about the Eighth Air Force's daylight bombing operations. Wyler and his team began their task late in 1942 but it was some weeks before a storyline was approved. The narrative was to be woven around a bomber crew's completion of a tour comprising the required 25 combat missions. Unfortunately, the first subject crew were shot down in April 1943 and interest then turned to Captain Robert K. Morgan and his men of the *Memphis Belle*, which Morgan had named after a girlfriend in that city. At the time it appeared that this bomber and crew would be the first in the Eighth Air Force to complete 25 missions and, unlike those of other contending B-17s considered, the name was unlikely to meet with any objections in the United Sates. In the event *Memphis Belle* flew its twenty-fifth mission on 19 May 1943 and the crew members on various dates during mid-May.

Memphis Belle was not the first B-17, nor were her crew the first crew, to reach 25 missions, but Eighth Air Force Public Relations could still justly say they were the first with 25 missions to be sent home to the United States. The documentary, which gave an account of the bomber's final sortie, was deftly handled and highly successful, both in dramatic form and in putting over the intended message. Wyler's daughter Catherine was sufficiently impressed by her father's work to enlist David Puttnam and Warner Brothers in making a fictional version which was shot in England in 1988, Duxford and Binbrook airfields being used for location work with seven surviving B-17s. The real *Memphis Belle* also survives, as a static exhibit on Mud Island at Memphis, Tennessee.

Robert Taylor has chosen to show *Memphis Belle* with landing gear down and flaps partly lowered on approach to a Bassingbourn runway on a late autumn day in 1942. A farmer and a villager glance up as their conversation is drowned out by the four Wright Cyclones. The countryside is very much akin to that part of Cambridgeshire, set beneath wonderful, wide East Anglian skies.

'The Other Half'

JOHN YOUNG

A TYPICAL East Anglian village panorama with a warplane rather than cattle occupying a pasture is not as incongruous as it may appear. So many airfields were created among the woods, fields and farmsteads of this region during the Second World War that it quickly became an accepted part of the general scene. The station buildings and hardstandings were woven into the normal rural features, soon making their aircraft, like this stoic B-17F, no more alien than a tractor or a threshing machine.

Once their tasks were completed, many 'fatigues'-clad ground crewmen made tracks through a gap in the boundary barbed wire to the local pub for a mild and bitter. Greene King is a Suffolk brewer, but there are many 'Crown' inns in that county and adjoining ones. The scene has a definite Sunday look, despite the fact that Monday was laundry day: in wartime, tradition and conformity were disregarded and hanging out the washing on the Sabbath could be overlooked. Some customs were not neglected: the old fellow seated at the far table wears his best suit and hat for his midday pint in the summer sun. What line of conversation holds with the two GIs and the middle-aged locals? The war? The weather? The contrasts of life in Britain and America? We can only guess.

Following a print-signing in Washington, DC, in 1978, the artist and his wife had lunch with two wartime commanders of the Eighth Air Force, Generals Doolittle and Eaker, at the Army & Navy Club. Ira Eaker enquired if his guests would refill their glasses with 'the other half'—an 'Englishism' that he cherished from High Wycombe days. This inspired John Young to use 'The Other Half' as the title for his painting of the American–British social gathering outside a village pub.

'The Deacon'

HOWARD GERRARD

HOWARD Deacon Hively was known to his compatriots in the 4th Fighter Group as 'The Deacon', and the nose of his second P-47 Thunderbolt was embellished with this name and an appropriate cartoon, A volunteer for service with the RAF, he joined No 71 Squadron in July 1942, transferring to the USAAF when this unit became 334th Fighter Squadron of the 4th Fighter Group in September that year. A year of operations passed before 'Deac' achieved his first aerial victory, but he went on to be credited with a total of 12 enemy aircraft shot down in combat and another two, plus a shared, credited while ground strafing. After home leave in the autumn of 1944 Hively resumed combat flying during the following winter until taking up a staff appointment at the end of January 1945.

During a bomber support mission over France on 15 June 1943 Hively's P-47 suffered an engine fire as a result of a hit-and-run pass by an unseen enemy aircraft. This resulted in 'Deac' having to bale out into the English Channel, whence he was extracted by the crew of a rescue launch and taken to Portsmouth. He was apparently little the worse for his experience since he even persuaded the crew to let him take the helm on the way back.

The second P-47 in Howard Gerrard's painting is the aircraft usually flown by another distinguished 4th Fighter Group pilot, Pierce McKennan, also an ace, with 12 air victories and nine ground strafing credits. McKennan flew two tours with the 4th and had a total of 560 hours' combat flying time. He was killed in a flying accident in 1947.

'The Regensburg Mission'

GIL COHEN

WE are inside the nose of *Just a-Snappin'*, the unofficial name bestowed on B-17F number 23393 of the 100th Bomb Group, as bombardier Lieutenant James Douglass signals the release of the bomb load over Regensburg. Lieutenant Harry Crosby, at his navigator's table, notes the time in the log: it is 1207, and the date is 17 August 1943. *Just a-Snappin'* is one of fourteen 100th Bomb Group Fortresses to reach the target; seven others that left England that morning have gone down. The signs of battle are the spent .50-calibre ammunition cases below the right cheek gun and fading smoke from flak bursts beyond the Plexiglas. A lull in the fighter attacks has allowed these two officers to go about their main duties.

The table has some of the tools of the navigator's trade, including a G-1 mechanical computer. Fixed above the bombardier's panel is a photograph of his wife. We see the other paraphernalia of a B-17 nose compartment—including the vital oxygen regulators, which must be constantly monitored because the onset of anoxia is not immediately apparent and when it comes it may be too late: the constant noise and vibration could have a soporific effect and lower one's guard.

Just a-Snappin' would survive this shuttle mission to North Africa, only to be shot up and wrecked after landing from a mission flown in early October. Harry Crosby eventually became Group Navigator, remaining with the 100th until the end of the war. He is said to have been the most highly decorated navigator to serve with the Eighth Air Force.

To ensure accuracy, Gil Cohen studied the nose compartments of two static B-17s in United States museums, backing this up with research on the equipment and fittings that were germane to *Just a-Snappin'*. After many preliminary sketches, Gil Cohen's technique, akin to that used by many of the classical masters, was to start with a basic drawing on the canvas, then apply a thin transparent underlay which did not obscure the outlines, and finally overpaint in oils. The result is atmospheric—one is right there in the action. Members of the Guild of Aviation Artists (British) voted this painting the best from a United States artist at the joint exhibition with the American Society of Aviation Artists staged at the US Air Force Museum at Dayton, Ohio.

'Scaling the Alps'

ROBERT BAILEY

AN Eighth Air Force unit that has legendary status is the 100th Bomb Group. This arose through its misfortune in suffering high combat losses on several occasions, earning the sobriquet 'Bloody Hundredth' and a reputation as a hard-luck unit among the personnel of other bomber groups. In fact, overall the 100th fared little worse than any of the other B-17 groups that entered combat in the early summer of 1943, but false reputations are not easily dismissed and the 'Bloody Hundredth' tag remained.

One of the first débâcles suffered by the 100th Bomb Group was on the so-called shuttle mission to bomb the Messerschmitt plant at Regensberg and fly on to land in North Africa on 17 August 1943. The 100th, positioned as the last formation in the bomber stream, sustained almost continuous fighter attack for two hours. Of the 21 Fortresses that had set out from Thorpe Abbotts that morning, seven had been shot down by the time the target was reached around noon and several others had been badly damaged , two so badly that they

made for neutral Switzerland after bombing. The remaining twelve followed the rest of the task force south, a move which at first confused the enemy defences for little opposition was encountered on the rest of the trip. Eleven hours after take-off the survivors reached North African airfields.

Robert Bailey chose the 100th Bomb Group's passage over the Alps in paying tribute to this famous operation. His painting depicts four of the survivors: Lieutenant Henry Hennington's *Horny*, Lieutenant Owen 'Cowboy' Roane's *Laden Maiden*, Lieutenant Robert Wolff's *Wolf Pack* and Lieutenant John Brady's *M'lle Zig Zag* (the lowest aircraft in the picture). During one of the attacks the wing-tip of an Me 109 struck the fin of *Wolf Pack*, leaving a considerable dent which made control difficult. The impact also opened the life-raft door and the released raft struck the fin. Of the four B-17Fs shown, *Wolf Pack* was the only one to survive combat operations and be returned to the United States, the others all being shot down later in 1943.

'After the Mission'

GIL COHEN

IN Gil Cohen's aviation art human beings take precedence over aircraft and inanimate images. His distinctive paintings also exhibit keenly observed detail that adds authenticity to the historical scene. Some studies are generic, like 'After the Mission', which could be at any one of two dozen Eighth Air Force bomber bases in eastern England during interrogation sessions.

The interrogating officer is an older man, perhaps an academic who lost no time in joining the Army Air Forces when America came into the war and became a group S-2 (Staff Intelligence Officer). Standing beside him is an almost stereotyped RAF officer, a man in his forties who saw service during the first 'do' and during the second has been given a liaison posting as RAF representative on a US bomber station. His presence at this crew's interrogation table suggests that this was the group lead crew for the mission—perhaps it is the 'Old Man' (Group CO) himself who points out a location on the map. Things went well, for he has a look of achievement on his face. The rest of his crew exhibit fatigue—understandably so after anything from six to ten hours of unceasing noise, cold and general discomfort.

Strong coffee brings relief, as do cigarettes (few young men were non-smokers in those days), so packets of Lucky Strike and Camel plus the Zippo lighter were commonplace on such occasions. One gunner has a bandaged hand. Frostbite? Or did he get caught in the mechanism when trying to clear a jammed round from his gun? It is late in the day and the lights burn. Also suspended from the curved ceiling of the Nissen building are aircraft models, and where the ceiling becomes the wall silhouette posters give additional shapes to aid aircraft recognition. The weary warriors look forward to 'hitting the sack': there may be another mission tomorrow.

'After the Mission' won 'Best of Show' at the 1994 exhibition of the American Society of Aviation Artists.

'Here Come the Marauders'

CHRIS FRENCH

THE Eighth Air Force is usually associated with the high-altitude, four-engine heavy bombers, the B-17 Fortress and B-24 Liberator. However, for eight months in 1943 twin-engine Martin B-26 Marauder medium bombers were assigned and some 250 on hand when the four groups flying them were transferred to the Ninth Air Force. The Marauder entered combat operations in May that year with two missions against a generating plant in Holland, flown at roof-top height. On the second of these all bombers were lost and low-level operations terminated thereafter.

In July the B-26 groups began operating at medium altitude—an optimum 10,000 feet—with considerable success, chiefly against enemy airfields within range of the bombers' Essex bases. The new Ninth Air Force was formed to support the cross-Channel invasion of the Continent planned for the following spring, and in mid-October 1943 the Eighth Air Force's Marauders were transferred to the Ninth's control.

One of the four B-26 groups, the 387th Bomb Group, was based at Chipping Ongar airfield, and Chris French's painting shows a squadron take-off on the main runway for a training mission in late July 1943. The view is to the north-east, with the road to Norton Mandeville in the foreground. The leading Marauder is *Mitch's Bitch*, a name derived from that of its original pilot. This aircraft was later to earn some fame among the men at Chipping Ongar airfield by returning from a combat mission and landing safely on one engine to help disprove the rumour that a B-26 would not stay in the air for long in such a condition. *Mitch's Bitch* came to grief in a crash-landing at base in May 1944.

'The Devil's Daughter'

GEOFF PLEASANCE

AGAINST a background of Germany's woods and fields, a B-17F Fortress of the 95th Bomb Group fights off Me 109s during a mission flown in the autumn of 1943.

During its combat service *The Devil's Daughter* was beset with mechanical failures, principally to engines and superchargers. The hydraulically actuated supercharger controls of the B-17F were prone to sluggishness in the extreme cold and humidity encountered in high-altitude flight over north-west Europe, particularly in winter. Supercharger failure meant loss of power, and a straggling bomber became vulnerable to enemy fighter interception. However, despite having had to abort (the colloquial Air Force term for failing to complete a sortie because of mechanical or equipment problems) on nine occasions, *The Devil's Daughter* completed 37 combat missions and survived enemy action.

A replacement aircraft, *The Devil's Daughter* was received by the 336th Bomb Squadron at Horham airfield in July 1943. Lieutenant Norman Rothschild and crew gave the bomber its combat début on the 24th, a long haul to Trondheim in Norway. Two days later, on what would have been its second mission, *The Devil's Daughter* had to abort owing to an oxygen leak. After a half dozen missions interspersed with mechanical failures, an emergency landing on a small landing ground at Headcorn, Kent, left it badly damaged and unable to return to Horham for a month. The squadron personnel obviously thought it would not return for, in its absence, they named a new B-17G replacement *Devil's Daughter the 2nd*. Lieutenant P. M. Dean's crew used the B-17F when it returned, and later it became a reserve aircraft because of its continuing engineering problems. On 8 March 1944 it should have been one of the 95th's aircraft bombing Berlin, but No 3 engine suffered an oil leak, causing the pilots to make an early return. Thereafter the base engineering officers declared *The Devil's Daughter* too war-weary for further attention and passed it on to a service depot. On 9 April 1944 the bomber began a flight back to the United States, where it later served in a replacement training unit. After the war the aircraft ended its days in the salvage depot at Ontario, California.

The 95th Bomb Group had the distinction of being the only group in the Eighth Air Force to receive three Distinguished Unit Citations, the most prestigious US honour bestowed on a military unit for an outstanding action. In recent times the group has been honoured again in that one of the US postage stamps commemorating the 50th anniversary of Second World War actions depicts B-17s displaying the 'B' in a square tail marking that was the 95th's identity symbol.

'Screamin' Mimi'

MIKE BAILEY

THE nosewheel tucks away as *Screamin' Mimi* lifts off Hethel airfield for a mission in the autumn of 1943. This B-24D was assigned to the 565th Bomb Squadron of the 389th Bomb Group, the third Liberator-equipped group to reach the Eighth Air Force, although its first missions were flown from North Africa while on detachment. The B-24D was notable for its 'glass house' nose in contrast to the gun-turret fixture of following models. The D model was generally pre-ferred by navigators and bombardiers for having more room, better visibility and the absence of strong draughts that entered round the turret sides. Pilots considered that it had better flight characteristics than the later models, not least for being some four to six thousand pounds lighter.

In the winter of 1943–44 a special organisation, the 801st Bomb Group (Provisional), informally known as 'The Carpetbaggers', was formed by the Eighth Air Force to conduct supply and agent deliveries to resistance movements on the Continent. Most of these operations were to be carried out under cover of darkness and the Liberator was considered the most suitable aircraft available for the task. Because the nose-turret B-24 models had such poor forward visibility, B-24Ds were preferred and in February 1944 *Screamin' Mimi* was transferred from the 389th Bomb Group to Burtonwood to be modified for these duties. During the course of the modifications the aircraft was given an overall coat of black paint, eliminating the nickname on the side of its nose. Delivered to the 36th Bomb Squadron at Harrington, the Carpetbaggers' base, B-24D 240997 was given a new nickname, *The Worry Bird*. On the night of 27–28 April 1944 the aircraft crashed into high ground at St Cyr de Valorges, about 25 miles west-north-west of Lyons, while on a supply-dropping mission. All but three of the crew were killed; one was taken prisoner and two evaded capture, helped by French patriots. The radio operator, T/Sgt James J. Heddleson, spent the next three and a half months working with the resistance move-ment and for his services the square in St Cyr de Valorges was renamed James Heddleson Square.

The name 'Screamin' Mimi' was derived from the original crew bombardier's habit of referring to his many hangovers as 'the scream-ing meemies'. Before leaving the United States in July 1943, this crew paid $50 to have the name and pink elephant insignia painted on the nose—only to have the aircraft taken away for use by the 389th Group on arrival in Britain while they were sent to the 93rd!

'The Odds of Valor'

MATTHEW WAKI

ARTISTS wishing to portray a specific incident have to conduct a certain amount of research, but few can equal Matthew Waki in dedication and extent. The subject of 'The Odds of Valor' is the air combat which brought the only Congressional Medal of Honor, the United States' highest award for bravery, to a fighter pilot in the European Theatre of Operations. On 11 January 1944 the Eighth Air Force launched a major mission against aircraft manufacturing targets in Germany. For the preceding three months weather conditions which could provide a good opportunity for visual bombing were rare, but on this day clear skies were forecast for much of north-west Europe. As so often happened, actual conditions were not as the prognosis. Cloud masses extending through several thousand feet were encountered over the North Sea and reports from task forces caused Command to issue a recall. However, the leading elements of two divisions, nearing their targets, found clear skies. The only escorts on hand to meet the heavy concentration of Luftwaffe fighters vectored to intercept the B-17s were 49 Mustangs of the 354th Fighter Group led by Major James H. Howard. Assigned to the Ninth Air Force, this, the first organisation to be equipped with the P-51B, the Merlin-engine version of the Mustang, was under the operational control of VIII Fighter Command.

Howard spread his force to give protection to as many of the bomber formations as possible, but the Mustangs were heavily outnumbered. In the ensuing combats Howard became separated from the rest of his flight and then spent the next half an hour intercepting enemy aircraft, attacking the bombers until only one of his guns was functioning. During this time he shot down two Me 110s and an FW 190, damaged two Me 109s and drove off other enemy aircraft by simulating attacks. Much of this action was observed by the B-17 crews who, on return to base, recommended a high decoration to acknowledge the selfless endeavours of Howard in affording them protection.

Before embarking on his evocation of this famous action, Matthew Waki went to great lengths to examine all relevant material. From various participants' reports he mapped the sequence of events before selecting that which he would depict. His choice was Howard's first victory, which was identified as a rocket-firing Me 110 of the 2nd Staffel of Zerstörergeschwader 26. Hit in both engines, the Messerschmitt took fire and went into a vertical dive. Very little is known about the Mustang Howard flew on this day other than that its identification letters were 'AJ:X'.

'The Courage of Eagles'

RONALD WONG

A FEATURE of many of Ronald Wong's paintings is a ghostly presence, often an aircraft forebear of an Air Force unit whose current equipment is the main subject. In 'The Courage of Eagles', the misty background presence is a representation of the national emblem of the United States. An unusual composition, the canvas depicts the two 303rd Bomb Group Medal of Honor airmen and the aircraft involved in the actions which earned America's highest award for valour.

1st Lieutenant Jack W. Mathis, in the top right-hand corner, was the bombardier of B-17F *The Duchess*, the leading aircraft of his unit's formation on a mission to bomb the submarine installations at Vegesack on 18 March 1943. As he bent over his bomb sight ready to make release, a flak shell exploded against the right side of the Fortress's nose, the blast hurling Mathis backwards and mortally wounding him. Despite horrific injuries to his right arm and body, he pulled himself back to the sight to release the bomb load. His dying word was 'Bomb…'; the navigator, seeing Mathis expire, added the crucial word 'away' to notify the pilot that their task had been achieved. *The Duchess* is shown as it appeared on this, its fourteenth combat mission, although the Fortress went on to survive another 45 before being retired and flown back to the United States.

The other aircraft, *Jersey Bounce Jr.*, was badly damaged by enemy fighters when returning from the Bremen raid of 20 December 1943. S/Sgt Forrest L. Vosler was wounded in the legs and abdomen by splinters from a 20mm cannon shell that exploded in his radio room. Vosler continued his duties, only to be struck by more fragments from a detonating cannon shell, this time around the face and eyes. Partially blinded, he still stuck to his post and when told that the bomber would have to be put down in the sea he rigged the emergency radio and transmitted distress signals. After the bomber ditched and while the crew were attempting to get into a liferaft, Vosler grabbed the incapacitated tail gunner as he slid off the wing. With a one-hand grip on the bomber's trailing aerial, he held the man in the water until other crewmen pulled them into the raft. All were subsequently rescued by a coaster. The bomber crew's praise for the conduct of their radio operator led to his receiving the Medal of Honor.

The Mathis and Vosler likenesses in the painting were skilfully captured by reference to the few photographs of these men that are available.

'Return to Halesworth'

GIL COHEN

GROUND crewmen are congratulating Captain Walker 'Bud' Mahurin after a successful sortie during which this Thunderbolt pilot claimed his eighteenth, nineteenth and twentieth victories, becoming the first fighter ace in the Eighth Air Force credited with twenty enemy aircraft destroyed. The date is 8 March 1944.

During his early days in England Mahurin had a narrow escape and earned the displeasure of his commanders through wrecking a P-47. This occurred when he flew too close to a Liberator and had the tail of his aircraft severed by one of its propellers. The B-24 kept flying, but Mahurin had to use his parachute. The replacement aircraft was a P-47 sponsored by the people of Atlantic City, New Jersey, through the purchase of war bonds to the value of the fighter. Nearly all of Mahurin's victories were obtained with this aircraft. He was flying it on 27 March 1944, his 85th mission, when the rear gunner of a Dornier Do 217 he intercepted put bullets into its engine. The P-47 went down. Mahurin evaded capture and, with the help of French patriots, eventually made his way back to England. Airmen who had been assisted in this way were not allowed to return to operations in the European theatre of war in case they were shot down again, captured and put under pressure to identify their helpers, and because of this ruling Mahurin had to return to the United States. Later he went to command a squadron in the south-west Pacific area, gaining another air victory, a Japanese bomber. He also flew in the Korean War and spent a uncomfortable period as a prisoner after being shot down.

'Texas Ranger and Friend'

MEL BROWN

THE personal Lockheed P-38J Lightning of Colonel Jack S. Jenkins, commander of the 55th Fighter Group, *Texas Ranger* was the first USAAF combat aircraft to fly over Berlin. This occurred on 4 March 1944 when Jenkins was leading a formation of P-38s assigned to give target support to the first US heavy bomber raid on the enemy capital. Mel Brown's painting shows Sergeant Robert Sand touching up the lasso of the design which he had painted at the Colonel's request.

The 55th Group's first combat equipment was the P-38H model, which was quickly superseded by the P-38J with better performance and range. As the *Texas Ranger*'s insignia was painted largely on the access panel over the gun bay, this panel was transferred to each new Lightning that the Colonel acquired.

The P-38s used during the winter of 1943–44, when the 55th entered combat, were found to be unsuitable for high-altitude operations because of the extreme cold and high humidity. The Allison engines were prone to failure on account of the low temperatures, and cockpit heating was insufficient. The P-38 also had restrictions on diving speeds, which hindered its combat performance. The aircraft was a delight to fly and an excellent gun platform, but its advantages were outweighed by the problems encountered and the type was eventually withdrawn from Eighth Air Force fighter squadrons.

Bob Sand, a quiet and sensitive man, was a member of the 38th Fighter Squadron propeller shop crew at Nuthampstead airfield, the setting for Mel Brown's painting. Apart from his artistic ability—he painted other personal markings on aircraft at pilots' requests—Bob was a highly competent photographer, producing a great number of images, both in colour and monochrome, of the English countryside and towns near his airfield bases. He also journeyed to other parts of Britain to make a unique photographic collection.

Although assigned to the Group CO, *Texas Ranger* was maintained by the 38th Fighter Squadron and carried its identification letters 'CG' and a white triangle. *Texas Ranger IV* was hit by ground fire while strafing Coulommiers airfield in France on 10 April 1944. Colonel Jenkins managed to crash-land his aircraft and escape little harmed, to be taken prisoner.

'Down at Denton Hill'

KEITH HILL

A FEW miles south-west of the city of Peterborough, the Great North Road—the A1—passes through the parish of Denton, a largely agricultural community. One of the landmarks to the west of the A1 is a small rounded rise surmounted by a copse. Here, on Sunday, 20 February 1944, a drama was concluded that led to the posthumous award of two Medals of Honor.

That cold and cloudy morning a B-17G of the 351st Bomb Group named *Ten Horsepower* took off from Polebrook to join a thousand other B-17s and B-24s dispatched on the first day of a determined series of strikes—later known as 'Big Week'—by the USAAF to cripple the German aviation industry. Lieutenant Clarence Nelson and his crew were late in joining the formation and became the target for an Me 109 pilot. Several cannon shells struck the forward fuselage, killing the co-pilot and causing horrific wounds to Lieutenant Nelson. *Ten Horsepower* immediately fell into a dive, but top turret gunner Sergeant Carl Moore managed to lean over the pilots and arrest the descent. The bombardier gave the order to abandon the aircraft and baled out, but navigator 2nd Lieutenant Walter Truemper, the only non-incapacitated officer left, took command, and Sergeant Archibald Mathies emerged from the ball turret and went to the aid of Truemper and Moore. He had a limited experience of flying, but after the body of the co-pilot had been removed he took the controls.

Radio contact was made with the control tower and the group CO advised the crew to bale out, setting the bomber on autopilot to head out towards the North Sea. The crew responded that Nelson was too badly wounded to use a parachute and that Truemper and Mathies would try to make a landing. Mathies made two unsuccessful approaches, and an attempt at nearby Molesworth, and he was then advised to return to Polebrook.

The damaged bomber approached Glatton airfield to the east of the A1, made a sweeping curve past the control tower, crossed back over the road and touched down in a large field. The airspeed was too high and, hitting rough ground, the B-17 cartwheeled and broke up. Mathies and Truemper were killed, but Nelson was still alive, though he died soon after he was pulled from the wreckage.

From 1983 to 1994 the USAF had an academy for its NCOs at RAF Upwood, some seven miles from the crash site. It was decided to name the Academy in honour of one of the four Second World War NCO airmen who were awarded their nation's highest decoration. The obvious choice was Archibald Mathies. This painting, commissioned by the Mathies NCO Academy, was based on the research of CMSgt David McClannahan and MSgt William McGelligot. It was displayed at Upwood until the Academy closed and it is now at the Gunter Annex, Maxwell AFB.

'Clash over Haseleunne'

ROBERT BAILEY

THE costliest mission undertaken by the Eighth Air Force was that on 6 March 1944 when 730 Fortresses and Liberators were dispatched to carry out the Command's first large-scale attack on Berlin. The German defences, responding in strength with flak and interceptors, were responsible for all but a few of the 69 bombers and 11 fighters which failed to return. On the other hand, the Luftwaffe fighter units suffered serious attrition with the loss of over 80 aircraft, many of the pilots being killed. The 100th Bomb Group earned its epithet 'The Bloody Hundredth' that day by losing fifteen Fortresses—half its force. After penetrating hostile airspace, the 92 mile-long bomber stream became separated in the middle and it was against the leading formations of the rear column that the German fighter controllers, sensing the absence of an escort, sent in a substantial force of interceptors. The 100th Group took the brunt of these attacks until a few P-47 Thunderbolts of the 56th Fighter Group came to their aid.

Canadian artist Robert Bailey shows 1st Lieutenant Robert S. Johnson's P-47 risking the defensive fire of the B-17s as he pursues an FW 190, which he shot down. The central Fortress is *Our Gal Sal*, piloted on this occasion by Lieutenant Robert Shoens of the 351st Bomb Squadron. This bomber was the only survivor of its formation to return to home base, although three others limped back to force-land elsewhere in England. Both the crew and *Our Gal Sal* endured, Bob Shoens finishing his combat tour in May 1944. *Our Gal Sal*, which had flown its first mission in late January that year, went on to fly more than a hundred by the end of hostilities.

Robert Bailey '94 ©

'Little Willie Coming Home'

KEITH FERRIS

ON 6 March 1944 Flight Officer Bernard M. Dopko's crew were assigned B-17G 42-37839 for a mission which proved to be the Eighth Air Force's first full-scale attack on the German capital. Apart from Dopko, who had flown an introductory mission with another crew, this was the third venture into hostile airspace for the other nine airmen who boarded '839' *Little Willie* that chill, dark morning. Their charge, however, was a hardened veteran of the air war over Europe, having been involved seventeen times since it was received by the 388th Bomb Group at Knettishall in the previous November.

Little Willie's flight was reasonably untroubled until over the target, when the two starboard engines began to falter, presumably from being struck by anti-aircraft shrapnel. The propeller on one started to windmill and had to be feathered, while the supercharger failed on the other. With this sudden loss of power *Little Willie* began to drop out of the formation. Dopko decided that the best chance of surviving the trip home was to go to low altitude, where power might be regained on the engine with the defunct supercharger and enemy fighters might be eluded. Almost immediately *Little Willie* was set upon by two enemy aircraft and cannon shells hit the tail, slightly wounding the gunner. Putting the bomber into a steep dive, Dopko was able to shake off the enemy, who probably thought the bomber out of control and doomed.

Recovering just above the treetops, the Dopko crew began the long haul back to England. Power returned intermittently to the engine with the blown supercharger, but airspeed was often dangerously low, averaging about 115mph as the Fortress struggled over towns and countryside at between 50 and 100 feet. Good fortune smiled, for little attention from the enemy was encountered until the Dutch coast was reached, where light flak was evaded. Some nine and a half hours after leaving, *Little Willie* put its wheels down on Knettishall's runway, the last bomber to return from the most costly mission the Eighth Air Force ever flew. A total of 69 B-17s and B-24s were lost that day, seven from the 388th Bomb Group whose formations had come under heavy fighter attack shortly after *Little Willie* had departed.

The damage to *Little Willie* was soon repaired, and three days later the Dopko crew and their bomber flew another mission to Berlin as a 'fill in' for another B-17 group. One engine was hit by flak and fire spread in the wing. Seeing that the bomber was doomed, Dopko ordered his crew to bale out and all ten men were taken prisoner. *Little Willie* crashed near Proetze.

Keith Ferris's atmospheric work in oils depicts *Little Willie* as it clears the dunes on the coast of Holland on 6 March 1944, the artist's skill brilliantly evoking the wild weather of that day.

'Mary Alice—Almost Home'

KEITH HILL

AGAINST a scene of the English countryside in the grip of winter, Keith Hill portrays the 401st Bomb Group's *Mary Alice* on its return from a rough combat mission. This B-17G, number 42-31983, was probably the most consistently major battle-damaged Fortress to serve with the Eighth Air Force. Delivered to the Group in early March 1944, being one of the last Fortresses in camouflage finish from the factory, it was assigned to 1st Lieutenant Dan Knight's crew. Dan named the aircraft in honour of his mother, Mary Alice.

This bomber carried the Knight crew through their tour, which was completed in late June, but not without collecting numerous perforations and a few in their persons from enemy fire. In July another crew brought *Mary Alice* back to England with a dead tail gunner following a battle with fighters. Repairs required a new tail turret.

Soon after returning to operations, the bomber was again caught by fighters and suffered more than a hundred shell and splinter holes with damage to major components. It was now the 'regular ship' of Lieutenant R. W. Callaway's crew, who flew it until late November when their 30-mission tour was completed. Lieutenant George Cracraft and his men inherited this worn sky chariot, which looked like 'a jigsaw puzzle' because of the many bright metal replacements. On their first mission *Mary Alice* suffered severe damage from closely detonating flak bursts, which wounded three of the crew. One of the injured was navigator Carl Hoag, who received the Distinguished Service Cross, the second highest US award for valour, for his conduct that day. It was also the only such award to go to a member of the 401st Group.

Yet again *Mary Alice* was patched up and put back on operations. Over Berlin flak again brought severe damage, and the bomber was nursed home on the power of three engines. On 16 February 1945 flak, once more the tormentor, crippled two engines and mangled part of the port wing and tail. Cracraft fully expected the bomber to be scrapped, but a month later, with three new engines and even more unpainted repairs, *Mary Alice* was back at its Deenethorpe base. The bomber flew its 98th and last mission on 19 April 1945, and despite the mauling it had received from the Luftwaffe it was deemed sufficently airworthy to be flown back to the United States.

In the 1970s the Imperial War Museum acquired a B-17 from France for static exhibition at their Duxford airfield site. This, a late production model that had seen no action and had been much modified for civilian duties, required extensive work to restore it to wartime configuration. The decor chosen for this exhibit was that of *Mary Alice*—which could not be a more fitting choice as an example of the durability of the legendary Flying Fortress.

'Riding High'

MIKE BAILEY

Two Boeing Fortresses of the 96th Bomb Group plough through a flak barrage on their way to a target. One is a B-17F model, the other a B-17G, the main visual difference between the two being the 'chin' turret of the latter.

The B-17G, officially serial number 42-31053, was named *Stingy* at the request of General Frederick Anderson, one time Eighth Air Force Commander for Operations, on behalf of his young son. *Stingy* came to the 338th Bomb Squadron at Snetterton Heath in the late autumn of 1943. During its service it was often used to lead the Group formation on combat missions. After completing more than fifty, on 9 October 1944, the aircraft was one of three Fortresses that collided during a training flight over Northamptonshire. Broken in two, the bomber fell to ground west of Towcester, all seven men on board being killed.

B-17F 42-30073, alias *Ole Puss II*, was a replacement for the original Fortress with that nickname that crash-landed at Grafton Underwood soon after the 96th commenced operations in May 1943. Assigned to the 413th Bomb Squadron, *Ole Puss II* was also used by the Group leader on several missions and survived many air battles, its gunners having claimed a dozen enemy fighters shot down by the spring of 1944. While on a local flight on 17 April there was an emergency due to loss of power and the bomber was wrecked while trying to land at East Wretham, but without hurt to the crew.

'The Jungle Princess'

JIM LAURIER

THE 392nd Bomb Group, based at Wendling, Norfolk, was the fourth Liberator group to reach the Eighth Air Force and the first to receive the Ford-built B-24H as original combat equipment. The H model introduced the Emerson power turret in the nose, but this Liberator had an all-up weight of 60,000lb, some 3,000lb heavier than the earlier B-24D, which made it difficult to handle in formation at altitudes above 20,000 feet. Eventually the Eighth Air Force introduced a weight-saving programme for Liberators and most aircraft had the retractable 'ball' under-turret removed. In Jim Laurier's painting the ball turret is prominent, its gunner dealing out 'point-fifty'-calibre rounds from the twin Browning machine guns at passing FW 190s. The 392nd Bomb Group formation is also encountering the black smudges of flak bursts as it heads for a target in Germany.

The 392nd Bomb Group began combat operations on 9 September 1943 and experienced severe losses during its early missions. *The Jungle Princess*, of the Group's 576th Bomb Squadron, survived these early raids, only to come to harm on a local flight. On New Year's Day 1944 an emergency landing at the RAF's Swanton Morley airfield resulted in the bomber ending up with a smashed forward fuselage.

'Milk Run'

NIXON GALLOWAY

THE structural integrity of the Boeing B-17 is famous. The bomber could continue to fly after its airframe had sustained extraordinary battle damage. Many examples of this durability are in evidence in photographs where B-17s have been brought back and landed with huge sections blasted away—noses forward of the cockpit, tail gunner's positions, entire tail stabilisers, an engine, or large parts of fuselage or wings gone. One of the most remarkable examples of this ruggedness was *Miss Irish*, a B-17G of the 350th Bomb Squadron, 100th Bomb Group. On 19 March 1944 Lieutenant John Gibbons and crew flew this aircraft as part of a force bombing a V-weapon site near Boulogne. As it only involved a brief penetration of hostile airspace over the French coast, the airmen looked upon the mission as a 'milk run', a colloquial term for an easy mission in comparison with what was usually faced when a target lay deep in Germany.

After the brief flight across the Channel *Miss Irish* was no sooner over the French coast when it took a direct hit in the radio compartment from an 88mm flak shell, the force of the detonation lifting the Fortress vertically several feet. The radio operator was killed and disappeared from the aircraft. When other crew members went to investigate they found that an enormous hole in the right side of the fuselage extended down into the bomb bay. Apart from a few tangled stringers, the rear portion of the aircraft was attached to the front only by the top and left side of the fuselage.

The Fortress was nursed back to England, where abandonment was considered but rejected owing to damaged parachutes. Despite severed cables, control was good enough for the pilots to believe a safe landing possible. The first airfield that came into view after crossing the English coast was Raydon, near Ipswich, occupied by a Ninth Air Force P-47 group. Only one attempt dare be made, and that with a gentle touch-down right at the threshold of the runway so that its whole length was available to lose speed: violent braking might cause the fuselage to split. Gibbons made a perfect approach and let the aircraft roll to a stop. *Miss Irish* was beyond economical repair, but until broken up and removed by the salvage men she was an object of much curiosity.

The gaping wound in the side of the Fortress, exposing the radio room interior, is not exaggerated in Nixon Galloway's painting. Other details in this realistic portrayal are the white trails of target smoke markers and the black smudges of the flak bursts bracketing *Miss Irish*.

'Chow-hound'

DAVID POOLE

FIVE members of a B-17 crew prepare to board *Chow-hound* for its 22nd mission while an officer is in the act of pulling himself up into the nose through the floor hatch. In full flying gear this demanded considerable effort and was left to the more athletic types. Most of the men whose stations were in the forward part of the bomber preferred the less strenuous, if longer-haul, approach, from the rear fuselage door through the bomb bay with its narrow walkway.

Chow-hound, with its Disney-type 'Pluto' motif, arrived in the 322nd Bomb Squadron, 91st Bomb Group, at Bassingbourn on 25 January 1944. It participated in most of the major missions undertaken by the Group during the following seven months until, on 8 August, it became a victim of anti-aircraft artillery fire when bombing enemy troop concentrations in France. The only loss from the 91st Group that day, *Chow-hound* crashed at Gelnannes. Also shown in David Poole's painting is the tail of veteran B-17F *Miami Clipper*, which was withdrawn from operations and returned to the United States in April 1944.

The artist was born in 1952 and studied fine art at Virginia Commonwealth University and the Corloran School of Art in Washington, DC. He commenced painting aviation subject matter full-time in 1980 and his commissions include work for Martin-Marietta, British Aerospace and organisations associated with the USAF.

'Buzzing the Tower'

HARRY CLOW

BUZZING was the word for a very low-flying pass. Unauthorised buzzing of an airfield usually brought a fine or some other penalty if the pilot responsible was apprehended. An exception was a crew's completion of a combat tour—25 missions to the spring of 1944, then 30 and finally 35 for those arriving during the final eighteen months of hostilities. It became almost a tradition that the final return to home base by the fortunate crew would be celebrated by a low pass over the control tower. Such was obviously the occasion for the crew in the Liberator buzzing the tower at Seething airfield, Norfolk, in the early spring of 1944, as depicted in Harry Clow's painting. B-24H number 252145, 'G-George' of the 712th Bomb Squadron, came to the United Kingdom with the 448th Bomb Group in December 1943 and endured nearly a hundred missions to be so battle weary that it was scrapped soon after the end of the war.

The control tower area at Seething is seen to be a veritable hive of activity . Two electricians work on the illuminated 'SE' , the visual airfield identification code, while in the background a Cletrac hoists a Pratt & Whitney engine and men work of the wing of a B-24 parked outside No 1 hangar. The control tower is the brick and concrete box type Air Ministry 12779/41, the standard building on most new airfields from 1943. To give the Flying Control staff better all-round visibility, a protective glass 'greenhouse' has been erected on the flat roof.

'Fighters Up'

JOHN CONSTABLE REEVE

PROBABLY the most eye-catching markings of all fifteen Eighth Air Force fighter groups were the black and yellow 'diamond' chequerboard engine cowlings of the 353rd Fighter Group's Thunderbolts. The paintwork was introduced in March 1944 and it took several days before all seventy-odd P-47s of the Group's three squadrons were so decorated. In April the 353rd moved bases from Metfield to Raydon and it is from the latter Suffolk airfield that John Constable Reeve portrays the Group's fighters climbing away for a combat mission. Raydon was built as a bomber base but never used for this purpose. At 150 feet, the runways were wide enough for two-plane elements of Thunderbolts to take-off together, thus hastening the assembly of formations.

The P-47Ds in the painting each carry two drop tanks beneath their wings, indicating a long-range mission. In the valley meadow scene a farmworker unloads fodder for cattle from a tumbrel. The motive power here required only vocal commands to move and stop—a distinct advantage over the tractor which would soon supersede the horse on East Anglian farms.

'Clash of Eagles'

ROY GRINNELL

THIS painting graphically illustrates an incident that occurred on the morning of 25 May 1944 when P-51s of the 336th Fighter Squadron were supporting B-17s bombing targets around the French–German border. They were intercepted by Me 109Gs of JG 1 with Oberfähnrich Hubert Heckmann of the 9th Staffel positioned behind and below the Mustang of Captain Joe Bennett. He then found that his guns would not fire, and in desperation the Luftwaffe pilot deliberately raised the nose of his Messerschmitt and let the propeller slash into the tail of the American aircraft. The impact caused the Mustang's tail assembly and rear fuselage to disintegrate and the bulk to nose up. Bennett was fortunate in being able to extricate himself from the cockpit and use his parachute before the stricken fighter fell on to a house in the village of Botenheim. Meanwhile Heckmann had managed to glide his badly damaged aircraft down to a successful belly-landing in a field. Bennett, a former RAF Eagle Squadron pilot, was taken prisoner and while in the local lock-up was visited by the Luftwaffe pilot who had brought him down in this unorthodox way. The 336th Fighter Squadron lost another Mustang in this fight but made claims of shooting down five of the enemy.

In Roy Grinnell's painting the crippled Me 109G6 dives away, its propeller blades bent, while P-51B 43-6572 sheds its rear end. Two other Mustangs can be seen in the distance and the winding Rhine below. The artist is renowned for his attention to detail and his endeavours to produce an accurate portrayal without compromising the artistic integrity of the complete painting. His skills have led Roy Grinnell to be appointed the official artist for the American Fighter Aces Association.

'Advance into Europe'

NICOLAS TRUDGIAN

HERE is an evocation of the early days of the invasion of Europe, with Republic P-47 Thunderbolts low over a liberated Normandy village. As with many of Nicolas Trudgian's paintings, this is a feast of detail: the typical village square with memorial cross, the *boulangerie* and café, the welcoming inhabitants and flags, a wrecked German tank and an array of US Army vehicles from Jeeps to Sherman tanks tracking between the damaged buildings of the narrow street. In the distance the smoke of battle and the waters of the English Channel can be seen.

The red noses of the Thunderbolts identify the famous 56th Fighter Group, the first American fighter organisation in the European theatre of operations to use bright colours for its units. Later several P-47 squadrons operating from the Continent also had red cowlings. The leading Thunderbolt is the personal aircraft of the legendary Hubert Zemke and was the first with a 'bubble' canopy, received by the 56th Group at its Boxted base. This aircraft was sponsored by the state of Oregon to serve with the USAAF flying from Britain through citizens acquiring War Bonds to the total cost of a P-47—a nominal $100,000. In recognition of this, Oregon's Britannia was painted on the left side of the fuselage.

When Colonel Zemke left the 56th Fighter Group the aircraft was taken over by Major Harold Comstock, formerly commander of the Group's 63rd Fighter Squadron. All seven Thunderbolts in the picture are from this squadron, bearing the distinguishing letters 'UN'.

'The Mighty Eighth—Russian Shuttle'

GIL COHEN

ON 21 June 1944 the Eighth Air Force flew its first shuttle to the USSR, bombing an oil installation at Ruhland near Berlin on the way and landing at the bases negoiated for such use with the Soviets. The plan was for the B-17s then to fly on to Italy, striking another target en route, and from Italy to return to the United Kingdom. Part of the fighter escort for this force accompanying the bombers to Russian territory consisted of four squadrons of P-51s, three from the 4th Fighter Group and one from the 352nd, amounting to 61 aircraft all told. The leader was the dynamic Colonel Don Blakeslee, CO of the 4th Group. Take-off from Debden was at 0755, and seven and a half hours later the Mustangs reached the assigned base at Piryatin in the Ukraine.

Gil Cohen has chosen to illustrate the moment when Don Blakeslee is pointing to his watch to show the Soviet officers who have come to meet him that he has arrived exactly at the predicted time. The enigma that was the USSR is well represented. True to custom, a bouquet is offered as a friendly greeting, while one Red Army officer loses no time in a close-up inspection of Don's Mustang and two other Russians act as if some intrigue is afoot. Perhaps these are the political watchdogs?

Gil's penchant for researching detail is apparent in this painting. Blakeslee, in common with many transferees from the RAF, preferred the British Mae West life-jacket and a British 'bobby''s whistle in place of the GI issue. Note also that the Colonel has flown wearing items of dress uniform and has already replaced his flying helmet with a service cap displaying his rank, all designed to impress the Americans' hosts.

A professional freelance artist and illustrator, Gil Cohen prefers to specialise in historical subjects. Apart from aviation, in which he is a contributor to the USAF Art Program, much of his work features American Civil War incidents.

'Salem Representative'

HOWARD GERRARD

AMORNING take-off from Debden, Essex, for an early fighter-bomber patrol on D-Day, 6 June 1944, is portrayed in Howard Gerrard's third rendering of a 4th Fighter Group subject.

Salem Representative was the assigned P-51B of the remarkable Ralph K. Hofer, from Salem, Missouri. The initial 'K' stood for Kidd and this soon led to Hofer's familiar tag as 'The Kid'. Flamboyant and irrepressible, Hofer had a reputation for 'doing his own thing', which led him to achieve 16 aerial victories and another shared, plus 14 aircraft destroyed on airfields in the dangerous task of low-level strafing. 'The Kid' shot down his first enemy on his first combat mission (8 October 1943), a unique event for an Eighth Air Force fighter at that time.

Hofer was killed in action on 2 July 1944 during the second stage of a shuttle mission, flying from the USSR to Italy. It is believed he fell victim over Yugoslavia to one of the Luftwaffe's great aces, the only high-scoring Eighth Air Force pilot to be lost in air combat. *Salem Representative* survived him, being out of commission when the flight to Russia was dispatched. This aircraft was notable for its white-painted sidewall tyres, a status symbol on pre-war American automobiles.

The other P-51 in the painting is Major Hively's, who led the 334th Fighter Squadron to the Rouen area to look for enemy movements. The 4th Fighter Group flew six separate formations on D-Day, claiming four enemy aircraft but losing seven of their own.

Artist Howard Gerrard trained as a professional illustrator and developed his interest in Second World War aircraft from a boyhood task delivering milk at the giant Burtonwood air depot near Liverpool. Every morning he had to negotiate piles of dismembered Mustangs, Thunderbolts and other types prepared for salvage.

'Old Crow'

JERRY CRANDALL

THE pilot of an FW 190 has jettisoned the canopy of his crippled aircraft and prepares to bale out. The main landing gear has come down, indicating a damaged hydraulic system, while flame and smoke comes from the engine compartment. Watching from the cockpit of his Mustang is Captain Clarence 'Bud' Anderson, whose accurate shooting brought about the demise of this Luftwaffe fighter. The occasion was an extensive air battle near Leipzig on 29 June 1944, when 357th Fighter Group pilots were credited with 21 enemy aircraft shot down for the loss of one their own while intercepting Luftwaffe attacks on heavy bombers. Bud Anderson shot down two other FW 190s this day to make his total of air victories 11, then the highest in the 357th.

All Anderson's Mustangs were named 'Old Crow', and that in Jerry Crandall's painting, the P-51B model, was his second. Although received at the 357th's base in bare-metal finish, the aircraft was given a coat of olive drab paint to make it less conspicuous on the ground, as were many other Mustangs at Leiston airfield. The fighter has a Malcolm hood, a British-made modification, giving better visibility from the cockpit. At the time of this air battle the camouflage was partly negated by full 'D-Day stripes' over wings and fuselage.

Clarence Anderson flew two tours totalling 116 combat missions with the 363rd Fighter Squadron of the 357th Fighter Group and had official credits for destroying 16.25 enemy aircraft in the air, the percentage resulting from a victory shared with three other pilots.

'Welcome Sight'

ROBERT TAYLOR

THE welcome sight in this scene is Ely cathedral, a very prominent landmark in the English Fens. The 900-year old building is an almost incongruous edifice in the sparsely populated, flat expanse of waterways, meadows and black-soil fields that stretch north from the city of Cambridge to the Wash. Nevertheless, it is one of the finest cathedrals in the United Kingdom and confers the title 'city' on the small fen market town. Built on one of the few islands of firm ground in the once extensive area of marsh and fen, this noble building became a ready point of reference for Second World War airmen. Visible for many miles and surmounted by a warning beacon, it often helped orientate pilots and navigators finding their home airfields.

The six Liberators in Robert Taylor's painting are passing over the River Ouse and the railway line to the east of Ely while heading for their base at Shipdham in west Norfolk. They are aircraft of the 44th Bomb Group's 68th Bomb Squadron, and *Corky*, officially B-24H tail number 251101, served with this unit from June 1944 until missing in action on 28 January 1945 during a mission to the oil installations at Kaiserstuhl. The bomber took a direct flak hit in the bomb bay and only the pilot, Lieutenant Maurice Corwine, and the radio operator survived from the crew of ten. *Corky*, then on its 65th mission, was named after the infant son of the squadron Operations Officer.

The 44th Bomb Group, which became known as the 'Flying Eightballs', was the first bomber group in the USAAF to receive B-24s and the second with the type to arrive in England. Its long commitment to combat, 30 months, accounts for its high losses of 153 B-24s missing in action during 343 missions. 'Welcome Sight' is in the collection of Dr. Robert Reid.

'U've Had It!'

MERLE OLMSTED

JOHN B. England was one of the outstanding fighter pilots of 357th Fighter Group, the first Mustang-equipped unit assigned to the Eighth Air Force and that which, during the final year of hostilities, had the highest success rate in air combats, resulting in its boasting more air aces than any other USAAF unit. John B. England had four personal Mustangs during his time with the 357th. The first of these, depicted in Merle Olmsted's painting, was named by the pilot after the British colloquialism of the time. In this case, 'You've had it!' was probably a tongue-in-cheek prediction that one's demise was inevitable in this aircraft, although the expression could mean, amongst other things, that something was not available.

U've Had It! carried John England safely through several combat missions, during which he shot down at least eight enemy fighters while at its controls. In the painting the aircraft is depicted as it appeared in June 1944, with the so-called 'D-Day stripes' of black and white around fuselage and wings. The symbols on the fuselage below the canopy record 25 escort and four fighter-bombing missions, plus nine aerial victories. Received with a bare metal finish in April 1944, this P-51B had its upper surfaces camouflaged green at the Leiston base to make it less visible when on the ground, enemy air attack still being a possibility. The fighter finally 'had it' early in October that year when it was wrecked by another pilot.

John England was promoted from 2nd Lieutenant to Major during some eighteen months' service with the 357th. He shot down his first enemy aircraft in March 1944 and went on to become the Group's leading ace for several weeks during the summer months, eventually being credited with 17 victories plus one shared with another pilot. A fighter pilot's tour was 300 hours' combat flying, but England managed to get his extended no fewer than five times, underlining his enthusiasm for the task, which had considerable risk. Like several other notable fighter pilots of the Second World War, he was to lose his life in a post-war flying accident. This occurred near Toul, France, when his jet fighter crashed in very bad weather on 17 November 1954. Later, the USAF named an air base in Louisiana in his honour.

'Destination Germany'

RONALD WONG

TWO 55th Fighter Squadron P-51D Mustangs climb away from a runway at the 20th Fighter Group's Kingscliffe, Northamptonshire, base in the summer of 1944. Both carry two 108 US gallon capacity 'drop tanks' under the wings, which allowed the Mustangs to provide escort for Eighth Air Force bombers to their furthest targets. The tanks were of paper/plastic composition, made by the Bowater organisation in the United Kingdom under a reciprocal agreement with US Lend-Lease aid to Britain.

The 20th Group converted to P-51s from P-38s in the summer of 1944 and the aircraft represented in the painting were two of the P-51Ds received at Kingscliffe in July when the Lightnings were relinquished. The Group's black and white banded nose markings were extended beyond the engine exhaust stacks at a later date but remained a somewhat sombre means of identification compared with the bright designs of the other fighter groups.

The Mustang marked 'KI:S' was flown by several pilots but mostly by 1st Lt Walter Mullins. Tragically, Mullins was killed in this machine when on a training flight over England in October 1944. The nearest Mustang, marked 'KI:Y', endured longer. 1st Lt William McGee was its pilot on 20 February 1945 when his flight was strafing an airfield near Nuremberg. The flight leader's aircraft was hit by ground fire but he managed a successful crash-landing in a large field. McGee decided to attempt to rescue his leader and appeared to make a successful landing. Unfortunately, the surface of the field was so soft that at the end of his landing run the main wheels began to sink, causing the aircraft to nose up and the propeller briefly to strike the ground. Undaunted, after discarding parachutes and other equipment, both pilots squeezed into the cockpit but by this time the Mustang was so badly bogged down it would not move. The two men had to abandon the attempt and make for nearby woods in the hope of avoiding capture. However, this was not to be and they were soon on their way to a prisoner-of-war camp.

The Jeep party is typical of pilots not scheduled to fly that day and who were sufficiently concerned for the well-being of their 'buddies' to wave the mission off. Sheepskin jackets were intended for use in high-altitude flight but were worn against the chill of an English morning.

'Dawn Chorus'

NICOLAS TRUDGIAN

THE tranquillity of an early June morning is broken by the deafening roar of a squadron of low-flying Lockheed P-38 Lightnings. The contrast between the traditional English riverside village and the thundering aircraft gives this scene such a dramatic atmosphere that some may question its validity: yet such occasions were most certainly common in 1944. Perhaps we are shown the early stages of departure for a combat mission over the Normandy beach-head—the fighters have the black and white 'invasion stripes' of that time—or, more likely, this is some low-flying, follow-my-leader practice in ground strafing techniques. The leader is Lieutenant-Colonel Cy Wilson, commander of the 55th Fighter Squadron, in his personal P-38J, *Wrangler.* The yellow propeller spinners and engine cowling rims identify the 20th Fighter Group of which this squadron was part,

based at Kingscliffe airfield, Northamptonshire. The polished nose tip and white backing band was intended to make it difficult for the enemy to distinguish between the normally armed P-38s and the special Plexiglas-nosed, bombardier-carrying version which was unarmed.

Nicolas Trudgian is noted for the diversity of his background details and this scene is no exception, with the village pub, red telephone box, an active wheel in the mill race and typical Northamptonshire stone bridge and houses, and with grazing cattle in the misty meadows warming under the rising sun. And there is a further reminder of the times—the American 'six by six' trucks marked with white stars in convoy, with the ubiquitous Jeep nearby.

'The Mighty Eighth—Outward Bound'

ROBERT TAYLOR

BLACK and white chequerboard markings were the hallmark of the 78th Fighter Group which occupied Duxford airfield, south of Cambridge, for nearly three years. Originally equipped with P-38 Lightnings, these and many pilots were taken as replacements for losses in North Africa before the 78th became operational. The Group then received P-47 Thunderbolts and used these in combat from April 1943 until the end of the following year, when it became the last Eighth Air Force fighter group to convert to Mustangs.

Robert Taylor's presentation is of Thunderbolts preparing to depart for a bomber escort from a grass airfield with a hard-surface taxiway. Full 'invasion stripes' on the aircraft indicate a date some time in June or early July 1944, which ties in with the established foliage of the trees. A P-47D taxies past while the pilots of two others await their turn to start engines, with ground crewmen in attendance. One of the latter has discarded his cycle in a hurry near a fire extinguisher. Each P-47 carries two 108 US gallon fuel drop tanks on its wing racks,

sufficient to give it a radius of action of up to 450 miles. The tanks were made in Britain, either of steel or a paper/plastic composition.

In the background are two visiting P-51s from nearby Bottisham, while overhead other 361st Fighter Group Mustangs from the same station climb away. The nose of another visitor, a P-38 Lightning, can be seen at the right-hand edge of the picture. Gracing the sky, further away, a B-17 squadron gathers a formation, obviously not part of the task force the chequerboard Thunderbolts will be supporting for their charges must already be heading towards hostile airspace. The East Anglian skyscape has heavier cloud towards the horizon, suggesting a day of sunshine and showers, and a puddle from recent precipitation is still in evidence in a perimeter-track depression. June 1944 was very much of this weather pattern. The often wet conditions at low-lying Duxford led its American tenants to christen the airfield 'The Duckpond'.

'Home Run'

ROBERT TAYLOR

THIS gorgeous rendering of a Mustang sweeping over a river exemplifies the skills that have seen Robert Taylor recognised as one of the world's foremost aviation artists. In this evocation one can almost hear the rasping roar of the Packard Merlin engine!

The location is a tributary of the Rhine flowing past a typical small Rhineland town. The period is the summer of 1944, and three Mustangs of the 361st Fighter Group are racing back to Bottisham, England, following an escort mission. The two leading aircraft are P-51D models with 'bubble' cockpit canopies, the third a P-51B with the high rear fuselage decking. The subject used for the main image is *Lou IV*, the personal aircraft of Group commander Colonel Tom Christian and the first 361st Mustang to have its yellow nose marking extended back to the cockpit to improve visual identification at long range. Tragically, Tom Christian was shot down in this aircraft by ground fire while engaged in dive-bombing a railway yard at Arras on 12 August 1944. *Lou IV* crashed at Boisleux-au-Mont and Christian died of his injuries the next day.

The painting was executed in 1990 to mark the fiftieth anniversary of the Mustang prototype's first taking to the air. The flight attitudes of the aircraft on the canvas were inspired by a film Robert Taylor had seen of civilian Mustangs in a recent air race at Reno, Nevada, dicing around a turn pylon at low altitude. The original canvas of 'Home Run' is in the collection of Dr and Mrs Jeffrey Walker.

'Zemke's Wolfpack'

ROBERT TAYLOR

AN evening spent in the company of Hubert Zemke inspired Robert Taylor to execute this work. Considered the best fighter leader in the Eighth Air Force by its commanding generals, 'The Hub', as he was known in VIII Fighter Command, led the 56th Fighter Group's pilots from inexperience to mastery, the Group having the highest total credits for air victories—667—of any fighter group flying in Europe as well as providing the two top-scoring aces, Robert S. Johnson and Francis S. Gabreski. Dubbed 'The Wolfpack', the 56th was responsible for many of the innovations in VIII Fighter Command and led the way in besting the Luftwaffe. Zemke always insisted it was very much a team effort and made plauditory comments on his successor, Dave Schilling, and on other senior officers.

'Zemke's Wolfpack' shows Hub Zemke leading a flight of 61st Fighter Squadron Thunderbolts in an effort to intercept FW 190s about to attack an ailing and straggling Fortress. The period of the action is summer 1944 and the nearest P-47D, number 226646, was usually flown by Lieutenant Sam Aggers at this time. This fighter was lost with another pilot during a fighter-bomber raid on 24 October the same year.

'Bridge Busting Jugs'

STAN STOKES

THE Republic P-47 Thunderbolt, designed as a high-altitude interceptor, was initially committed to battle in a bomber support role. Being almost twice the size and weight of the enemy fighters it was pitted against, the P-47 proved to have an inferior rate of climb and poor acceleration in comparison. Nevertheless, by utilising its advantages—high speed at high altitude, an excellent dive performance and heavy firepower—the Thunderbolt was used most effectively in this role. With a large tactical fighter force being formed to support the cross-Channel invasion of mainland Europe, the USAAF found an even more promising use for the Thunderbolt. Its armament of eight heavy machine guns, plus underwing and underfuselage shackles that allowed a load of 2,000lb of bombs to be carried, made this fighter excel in ground-attack duties. Additionally, its heavy construction and radial engine proved able to absorb battle damage that would have brought down a less hardy machine. The P-47 became the mainstay of the US Ninth Air Force that supported the armies in their battles from Normandy to the Elbe.

The Eighth Air Force also utilised its remaining P-47 groups for ground attack when not required for bomber support. Stan Stokes depicts Thunderbolts of the 61st Fighter Squadron, led by ace Francis Gabreski, in the act of demolishing a river bridge with 500lb bombs. Such small targets were difficult for high- or medium-altitude bombers to hit, whereas fighter-bombers could usually destroy these objectives in dive attacks.

However, important bridges, usually well defended with light anti-aircraft guns, took a goodly toll of Thunderbolts at low level. Lieutentant-Colonel Francis Gabreski was lost trying to avoid murderous flak while engaged in ground attack. He was at the time the highest-scoring fighter ace in the Eighth Air Force. He survived as a prisoner-of-war and added to his achievements in the Korean War. With a total of some 34 air victories he became America's most successful fighter ace extant.

'After the Storm'

JOHN YOUNG

WITH No 4 feathered, and shooting red distress flares to indicate wounded aboard, a silver 'B-17G comes into land at Ridgewell, Essex, following a combat mission. Perhaps it was 20mm cannon shells from a fighter pass, but more likely the steel splinters from a nearby flak burst, that caused the bomber to limp home. The date is some time in the autumn of 1944 on an afternoon when storm clouds add to the pilots' problems. In the foreground a Fortress, having returned from the same raid, waits on the perimeter track to cross the runway head to its parking place. The inner engines are already shut down as only Nos 1 and 4 are required for forward motion, the aircraft manoeuvring by increasing or decreasing the power of each. This Fortress, tail number 297503, was named *Princess Pat* and was assigned to the 381st Bomb Group's 533rd Bomb Squadron early in 1944. It completed well over one hundred missions in a year of combat. While on a local flight on 27 March 1945 it developed mechanical problems, crash-landed at its home base and was burnt out, the crew having escaped unharmed. The 'L' in a triangle on the tailfin was the 381st Bomb Group marking.

'The Mighty Eighth'

JOHN CONSTABLE REEVE

JOHN Constable Reeve combined a seven-day week as a Suffolk dairy farmer with an artist's pallet for more than forty years. Most of his canvases are pastoral scenes, but an interest in aircraft has led him to paint a number of subjects associated with aviation. In 1978 a friend commissioned him to produce a large canvas depicting the morning departure of Eighth Air Force bombers and fighters on an offensive mission. The picture was based on the friend's vivid memory of a cold and cloudless morning in early 1945 when a thousand bombers passed overhead, three to four miles high, as they made for their point of departure on the Suffolk coast. The result, in oils, is 'The Mighty Eighth', a scene based on the location of the friend's 1945 viewpoint but transferred in time to the late autumn of 1944.

In the foreground two farm hands look up from their labours loading mangolds into a trailer towed by a Fordson tractor. Behind them is the vista of the Stour valley with the golds and browns of autumn leaves. The main players are the bomber formations, their vapour trails curving through the heavens as they manoeuvre for position before heading out to the North Sea. At lower level some of their protectors, the fighters, have risen from a nearby airfield. They are Thunderbolts in the colours of the 61st Fighter Squadron.

Despite his Christian names, John Constable Reeve is not related to the famous nineteenth-century landscape painter. His father, also with artistic talent, was a great admirer of John Constable and chose to name his son in the luminary's honour.

'Colonel Donald Blakeslee'

FRANK BERESFORD

FRANK E. Beresford was born in Derby, England, in 1881 and his artistic abilities led to a career in which he specialised in portraiture. He was an admirer of the Dutch Masters, and much of his work between the wars was done in the Netherlands, where he was honoured by the Royal House. His reputation led to commissions to paint the rich and famous, including British and foreign titled individuals.

Early in the Second World War Frank Beresford was approached by the Minister for Air and asked to record the activities and personnel of RAF squadrons. For several months he stayed with various units, notably Dutch and Polish, and then visited the Eagle Squadrons with their American volunteers. When the USAAF arrived in the United Kingdom, through friendships established with American officers, he turned his attention to painting portraits of their distinguished airmen and general scenes at bases. The USAAF authorities in Britain were so impressed with Beresford's work that in July 1943, in order to facilitate further studies, he was granted credentials as an accredited US War Correspondent, No 1242. His prolific works in this area led many people to think he was a US national—a belief sustained by the fact that the United States Air Force Art Program has acquired 55 examples of his paintings. After the war Frank Beresford turned his talents to illustrating the Dan Dare strip in the *Eagle* comic. A founder member of the Society of Aviation Artists, Beresford retired to live in Sussex, where he died in 1967.

One of the many fine portraits of Eighth Air Force personnel painted by Beresford is this 1944 rendering of Colonel Don Blakeslee in the cockpit of his Mustang. Blakeslee was one of the most colourful fighter pilots in the Eighth Air Force and led the 4th Fighter Group at Debden to great achievement. A volunteer for the Royal Canadian Air Force, he served with Nos 401 and 411 Squadrons before joining the RAF's No 121 Eagle Squadron, a unit that was transferred to the USAAF to become the 335th Fighter Squadron of the 4th Fighter Group. Acknowledgement of Blakeslee's former service is carried on the motif at the top left hand corner of the painting, which included the badge of No 121 Squadron.

'Combat for a Straggler'

KEITH HILL

ALONE B-24J Liberator of the 466th Bomb Group fights off the attentions of Messerschmitts. Such a situation did not bode well for a comparatively slow, four-engine aircraft, although there were instances of solitary B-17s and B-24s surviving the hail of 20mm cannon shells and machine-gun bullets that were aimed at them. The best hope of survival was to seek the shelter of a cloud, and the pilots of the Liberator in Keith Hill's painting are probably intent on doing just that. The feathered propeller on No 4 engine adds to the predicament of the crew, although the B-24's nose gunner has disabled one enemy fighter.

A straggler from a bomber formation was usually in peril, but this one endured. The Liberator's markings identify it as number 44-40253 of the 787th Bomb Squadron, which entered service with the 466th Group in the autumn of 1944 and returned to the United States in May 1945. Nicknamed *Hard Luck*, it was often flown by Captain John Woolnough's lead crew.

As a retiree, in the early 1970s John Woolnough founded the Eighth Air Force Historical Society, the veterans' organisation that had some 20,000 members during the following decade. Keith Hill, a former ambulance man who painted as a hobby, was commissioned by the Eighth Air Force Museum and Memorial Foundation, an off-shoot of the veterans' organisation, to produce 58 paintings each featuring a representative aircraft of a different Eighth Air Force group.

'The Memorial Chapel'

FRANK BERESFORD

FRANK Beresford's prolific wartime art included several paintings made with the 96th Bomb Group at Snetterton Heath, Norfolk, of which that adjudged the most popular with its personnel was the airman kneeling in St Mary's Chapel at Quidenham Church.

The airfield's domestic sites were situated close to Quidenham parish church and the vicar, the Reverend William Harper-Mitchell, quickly established a rapport with the Americans on their arrival in the spring of 1943. The interchange of religious activities resulted in 96th Group personnel developing a kindly attachment to ancient St Andrew's. In April 1944 a squadron flight surgeon, Captain Herbert Allen, proposed that the men of the airbase fund a memorial window in St Andrews if this was acceptable to the church authorities. The Reverend Harper-Mitchell eagerly embraced the idea and after some discussion the restoration of St Mary's chapel within the church as a gift from US servicemen to the parish was approved. The sum of £597 for the refurbishment and a stained glass window established, and

problems with wartime building restrictions overcome, the work was put in hand. The window featured an airman looking up at Christ with surrounding embellishments that included the unit insignia of the Group and its squadrons, and a formation of Fortresses.

The rejuvenated chapel and window installation were dedicated in November 1944 and represented the first memorial to an American Air Force unit within an English church. Several other memorial windows acknowledging the sacrifice of US flyers have been installed in British churches during the past half-century, but Quidenham's is the only one dating from the war years.

When Frank Beresford was moved to record St Mary's Chapel on canvas, he wanted to include an American airman at prayer. As none was present when he set up his easel in the church, he asked a local man, Tony Green, who was tidying the churchyard, if he would pose for him in the required position. The touching result of Beresford's skills is now held in the US Air Force Art Collection.

'Top Cover'

DEREK BUNCE

DEREK Bunce's career as an illustrator with the British aviation industry explains his firm understanding of aircraft, so clearly visible in 'Top Cover'. This dramatic painting depicts Thunderbolts of the 84th Fighter Squadron weaving over a B-24 Liberator formation in the act of penetrating enemy airspace. The black and white chequerboard of the Duxford-based 78th Fighter Group has attracted several aviation artists, and Derek Bunce's foremost Thunderbolt displaying this engine cowling group identification marking was the assigned aircraft of First Lieutenant Frank Oiler. The fighter was named *Eileen,* and this appellation was painted on the left side of the fuselage. Oiler survived his combat tour of 300 hours' operational flying and returned to the United States in the early spring of 1945. His P-47D, tail number 228878, was transferred to a Ninth Air Force fighter group on the Continent when the 78th converted to Mustangs, and the aircraft was lost in action during April 1945.

The B-24 formation is that of the 489th Bomb Group, which was based at Halesworth until selected as the first Eighth Air Force heavy bomber group to be removed from operations for return to the United States. It ceased combat missions in November 1944 and was training with B-29 Superfortresses for operations against Japan when hostilities ceased.

'Miss Ida Comes Home'

MEL BROWN

THIS painting, by a young Texan artist, was originally commissioned by the 457th Bomb Group Association and presented by its members to the USAF Academy at Colorado Springs. It is currently displayed in that establishment's Arnold Hall.

Miss Ida, official number 44-8152, was a B-17G assigned to the 457th Bomb Group's 748th Bomb Squadron. The 'U' in a triangle and blue diagonal band on the vertical tail were the Group's markings, while blue-painted propeller bosses identified the 748th Bomb Squadron. The bomber was equipped as a 'pathfinder', having H2X ground-scanning radar, the scanner being housed in the retractable opaque dome substituted for the under-turret amidships.

Received by the Group in September 1944, *Miss Ida* flew many squadron and group lead positions and on occasion received a number of flak splinter perforations. It was not the enemy but mechanical failure that brought about the bomber's demise. Near the end of the war, on 5 April 1945, *Miss Ida* took off in pre-dawn darkness as the lead plane on a mission to Ingolstadt. An engine caught fire during the climb-out, causing the heavily loaded aircraft to crash in a ploughed field about a mile from the runway. Nine of the ten men aboard, including the 748th Bomb Squadron CO, Major Ed Dozier, were killed. The lone survivor was a navigator, Lieutenant Willing Meng, who was thrown clear during the initial impact: though severely injured, he recovered.

The background scene depicts the technical area of Glatton airfield with its workshops and one of the black T2 type hangars, the standard on late wartime bomber stations. Before the control tower, on the left of the picture, is the signal square with the letters 'GT', the visual identification code for Glatton. Beyond the airfield the distinctive tower of Conington village church can be seen, a familiar landmark to crews of the 457th Bomb Group. In fact, Glatton airfield was built largely within the parish of Conington, bordering the eastern side of the A1 highway. The village of Glatton was on the western side of the Great North Road, its name being used as the official name for the airfield to avoid confusion with the existing airfield at Coningsby some miles to the north.

'Horsham Pair'

MIKE BAILEY

TWO Liberators of the 458th Bomb Group which survived hostilities and were flown back to the United States in May 1945. *Old Doc's Yacht* served with the 754th Bomb Squadron for a year at Horsham St Faith (now Norwich Airport) and at the end of the war was credited with having completed more combat missions than any other B-24 still flying with the 458th Group—a total of 104. In contrast to the worn camouflage of this B-24H model, received as a replacement in April 1944, the far aircraft in shiny natural metal finish is a B-24L equipped with radar devices for pathfinder duties. The latter B-24 entered service at the end of 1944. Wearing the markings of the 755th Bomb Squadron and a saucy nude motif, its name, *Oh Mona!*, was probably derived from the title of a popular song of the time.

Old Doc's Yacht is of special significance to artist Mike Bailey. As a 10-year old who regularly squeezed through the boundary hedge at Horsham St Faith and was tolerated by the ground personnel, Mike often played in and around this bomber. As uncautioned small boys were wont to do in those days, he occasionally came away with dangerous souvenirs hidden under his jacket such as signal flares! These early encounters with Liberators left him with a permanent and obsessive love of the type which he has presented in many of his paintings. He declares that his greatest thrill was being allowed a flight in the Confederate Air Force's Liberator *Diamond Lil* when it visited the United Kingdom in 1992.

'One of Four that Day'

ROY GRINNELL

CHARLES 'Chuck' Yeager has his place in aviation history as the first person to exceed the speed of sound in an aircraft. Not so well known is his previous career as an Eighth Air Force fighter pilot. A member of the original pilot complement of the 363rd Fighter Squadron, 357th Fighter Group, that arrived in Britain at the end of November 1943, he was shot down by enemy fighters on 5 March 1944, parachuting safely although wounded in both feet. Evading capture and sheltered by the French underground movement, Yeager finally made his way back to Britain after some further narrow escapes.

In order to protect French helpers, an airman who had evaded capture with their aid was not permitted to resume flying combat sorties in Europe, lest he be shot down again and succumb to identifying his benefactors. When Yeager was able to return to combat that ruling no longer applied as most of France had been liberated. Back in action, he was credited with five Me 109s in a formation surprised on 12 October, and on 27 November, a day the Luftwaffe put up very large formations to meet Eighth Air Force operations,

Yeager shot down four enemy aircraft. In total he was credited with 11 1/2 air victories.

Roy Grinnell has chosen to depict an incident during the air battle of 27 November 1944. On this occasion the 363rd Fighter Squadron was flying top cover for other fighters detailed to strafe targets in the Magdeburg area when two huge formations of enemy fighters were reported. The squadron leader, Major Clarence Anderson, told Captain Yeager over the radio to lead the attack as his flight was better positioned. Yeager climbed above the larger formation before initiating his attack from 32,000 feet. The rearmost aircraft, an FW 190, rolled right into a dive and then pulled up into a tight turn to the right. Yeager opened fire with a deflection shot at the FW 190 and from 200 yards hit the rear fuselage. The FW 190 rolled and as it did so the tail broke off. The painting shows the moment the FW 190 came apart and Yeager's Mustang, *Glamorous Glen III*, pulling up. Yeager went on to shoot down another three FW 190s during the next five minutes.

The copyright of 'One of Four that Day' is held by the American Fighter Aces Association.

'Ruby's Fortress'

STAN STOKES

IT has been estimated that some seventy-five per cent of the unofficial paintings on Eighth Air Force aircraft featured the female form. Command turned a blind eye to this frivolity, believing that it helped morale, and only ordered the removal of that considered too outrageous or veering towards the obscene. Most of these representations were of nudes or scantily dressed forms. An exception was the painting on *Ruby's Raiders*, a B-17G of the 550th Bomb Squadron, 385th Bomb Group, based at Great Ashfield, which featured a portrait of an attractive US servicewoman. This was the result of a competition organised by the United Kingdom office of the US forces' newspaper *Stars and Stripes* in the winter of 1944–45 to find the most beautiful WAC in Britain. Nominations were open to all US servicemen. The girl finally awarded this compliment was Private First Class Ruby Newell, who served at divisional headquarters—all US servicewomen were employed at higher headquarters and none were on operational stations. It was arranged for Corporal Bill Ploss, an able artist at Great Ashfield, to paint a portrait of Pfc Newell on the side of B-17 number 46483 and to add the name *Ruby's Raiders*. When it was completed, Ruby, whose home was in Long Beach, California, was brought to Great Ashfield to pose with her likeness so that the Press could take photographs.

Ruby's Raiders served her aircrews well, flying some fifty missions and surviving hostilities to be returned to the United States. Stan Stokes' painting depicts this Fortress fulfilling the role it was designed to meet.

'Daylight Raid over Germany'

FRANK WOOTTON OBE

AGAINST a pall of acrid smoke from a burning target, Fortresses start the run home to England; in the background Mustangs deal with Focke-Wulfs. The B-17s carry the 'A-in-a-triangle' marking of the 91st Bomb Group, probably the best-represented of all Eighth Air Force groups in works of art. This painting was used as a poster for the artist's exhibition of 56 paintings held by invitation at the Smithsonian National Air and Space Museum, Washington, DC, for twelve months from September 1983.

Frank Wootton has been called 'the grand old man' of aviation art, for his name has been synonymous with aircraft paintings for more than half a century. An anecdote from another artist whose work is featured in this book illustrates this renown as being long established. In October 1944 US serviceman Brooks Whelan was stationed at Leominster: 'One day a buddy and I borrowed a couple of bikes and took a tour of the area. Somewhere in the vicinity there was an airfield which we accidentally came across. It was surrounded by a fence complete with guard house, etc. I noticed a British airman some distance away inside the fence sitting on the ground near the end of a runway sketching something but I am not sure what. I approached the guard and asked him what the airman was doing. He answered, and I don't remember the exact words, it was "some crazy artist drawing pictures of planes" in a tone of voice and with a facial expression that implied grown-ups should have better things to do with their time. Being an artist myself, I enquired whether he, the guard, knew the artist's name, and his reply was "Wootton, or something". Shortly after, I got a pass to London and bought Wootton's book *How To Draw Planes*, which I carried with me through the rest of the war and still have in my library. You might say it was an early inspiration in my career.'

'Prelude to a Mystery'

DOUGLAS ETTRIDGE

AT 1355 hours on 15 December 1944, Major Alton G. Miller, leader of the American Band of the AEF, left Twinwood Farm airfield for a flight to France and was never seen again. The loss of the world famous musician has been the subject of great interest and much speculation ever since. Several theories have been advanced as to the reasons for the disappearance of Glenn Miller, ranging from the absurd to those worthy of serious consideration. However, all that is really known is that he was a passenger in Noorduyn UC-64A Norseman transport aircraft 44-70285 which crossed the south coast of England and was never reported making landfall on the Continent. The weather was extremely cold and the crews of other aircraft reported icing conditions at low altitudes over the Channel. The Norseman did not have de-icing equipment and the most probable explanation of loss is that carburettor or some other form of icing was encountered that took the aircraft down into the sea where the chill water would soon take the lives of any survivors.

In Douglas Ettridge's representation of the scene at Twinwood Farm shortly before the fateful departure, Glenn Miller talks with Lieutenant-Colonel Norman F. Baessell, a fellow passenger, and the pilot, Flight Officer J. R. S. Morgan. Twinwood Farm was an RAF station used by the nearby US Air Service Command headquarters for communications flights and was also close to the Band's Bedford base. After some forty performances at US military installations during the summer and autumn of 1944, the band was moving to France, the main party flying in C-47 transports. Major Miller did not care for flight in the C-47 and took up an offer to be flown over in the Norseman to Villacoublay near Paris. The Canadian-built eight-seater was widely used by the USAAF for communications work and was considered sturdy and reliable; but the elements could precipitate the loss of any aircraft.

This painting is in the collection of Mr and Mrs Richard Artz.

'George Preddy'

JIM LAURIER

GEORGE E. Preddy was the most successful of all P-51 Mustang fighter pilots if air victories alone are the yardstick of assessment. His total of 26.83 enemy aircraft shot down was calculated officially, but other assessments credit him with higher figures and one study with a round 28. He was undoubtedly the epitome of a successful fighter pilot—aggressive and determined, with a singleness of purpose. An excellent pilot, his better than average eyesight and fast reactions made him a formidable opponent. However, he was a sensitive man and was considered an intellectual by some who knew him.

Preddy's first combat service was flying Curtiss P-40s in defence of Darwin, Australia. Here he had no opportunity to shoot down the enemy and was fortunate to survive a mid-air collision with another pilot during a training flight. Returned to the United States, he joined the 352nd Fighter Group and came overseas with it in the summer of 1943. At the end of January 1944 George Preddy had to bale out over the Channel when his P-47 was hit by flak. Despite the extreme cold of the sea at that time of year, when death through exposure is but a matter of ten minutes, he managed to climb into his dinghy and after an hour was finally rescued by an RAF Walrus amphibian, little the worse for his experience.

His first two victories were achieved flying a Thunderbolt, but it was with the Mustang that Preddy really excelled. On 6 August 1944, while escorting B-17s, he led his flight to intercept a formation of 30 Me 109s. In the next few minutes Preddy shot down six of the enemy and brought back gun camera footage to prove it.

In Jim Laurier's portrayal of this distinguished fighter pilot, George Preddy is in the cockpit of his Mustang with the familiar grin that distinguishes most photographs of this brilliant young man.

'George Preddy's Last Chase'

JIM LAURIER

APROFESSIONAL artist and illustrator who can turn his hand to any subject, Jim Laurier is never happier than with people and planes. 'George Preddy's Last Chase' fulfils a wish to acknowledge a tragedy. The word 'tragedy' is appropriate for many aspects of war, but it is particularly appropriate to the loss of Major George 'Ratsy' Preddy on Christmas Day 1944.

At the time Preddy was the leading ace of the Eighth Air Force in aerial victories and on his 143rd combat mission. The air echelon of his group, the 352nd, had moved from Bodney, England, to Asch, Belgium, two days earlier as part of the air reinforcements to meet the crisis that had arisen through the Germans' offensive in the Ardennes. The 352nd Fighter Group was tasked with always having one of its squadrons airborne and patrolling specified areas near the battle lines during daylight hours.

Commanding the Group's 328th Fighter Squadron and flying his personal Mustang, George Preddy shot down two Me 109s in a dogfight near Coblenz and with his wingman, Lieutenant James Cartee, pursued a low-flying FW 190 south-west of Liége. The Focke-Wulf flew west, skimming over the forest. In the speed of the action an American anti-aircraft unit fired on the enemy aircraft with light arms and then mistook the pursuing Mustangs also as hostile types. Both were hit, and Preddy's aircraft crashed in the field where the AA guns were sited, disintegrating on impact. In the painting the two blue-nose Mustangs begin their pursuit of the FW 190 over the snow-laden conifers of the Ardennes.

At the time of his death George Preddy had flown over 500 hours of combat time. Preddy's brother William, who also flew Mustangs with the Eighth Air Force, was killed in action in April 1945.

'Clearing & Colder'

JACK OLSON

IN 1985 the Boeing Company celebrated the fiftieth anniversary of its most famous product, the Flying Fortress, taking to the sky for the first time. As part of the programme of events at Seattle, the aircraft's birthplace, Boeing commissioned staff artists to produce a series of paintings to mark the occasion. Jack Olson's contribution was 'Clearing & Colder', which depicts B-17G tail number 338658 of the 601st Bomb Squadron, 398th Bomb Group, parked at wintery Nuthampstead. Perhaps his choice of subject may have been influenced by Ted J. Johnston, who was entrusted with the organisation of the 1985 anniversary proceedings by Boeing, for he had served as a pilot with the 398th Group in England. However, 'Clearing & Colder' proved very popular and was reproduced as a successful print by the Seattle Museum of Flight, who now hold the original. Artist Jack Olson, a former Eighth Air Force B-24 pilot, has deftly incorporated his 'trademark' as in most of his paintings—a small fieldmouse, which can be seen in the foreground snow.

Fortress 338658 sampled flak on several occasions. During its five-month combat career it was twice down at the emergency landing ground at Woodbridge requiring extensive repairs. On Friday 13 April 1945 this bomber was one of ten squadron aircraft unloading ordnance over Neumünster's rail marshalling yards when two of the RDX bombs touched in a mistaken salvo release from the deputy leader. The resulting explosion damaged nearly every B-17 in the squadron, three so badly that they were abandoned by their crews; two others brought down in liberated territory were write-offs, the subject aircraft being one of them. Two of the crew had been wounded, but all escaped after pilot Ray Herden crash-landed the crippled bomber, which was then almost completely destroyed by fire.

'High Gs on the Deck'

BROOKS WHELAN

ON 29 January 1945 a flight of four 338th Fighter Squadron Mustangs, led by 1st Lieutenant Roy D. Miller, was looking for targets in north-west Germany after providing escort for a bomber mission. About 50 miles north-east of Hamburg, 1st Lieutenant Walter J. Konantz , flying the No 3 position, called out that there were three 'bogeys' at 11 o' clock level, headed north-west, about five miles distant. None of the other pilots could see them, so Konantz assumed the lead and began closing on the three aircraft, which were soon identified as Me 109s. Konantz saw that the leading Messerschmitt carried an external fuel tank. He opened fire, hitting the tank, which was promptly jettisoned. The other two Me 109s broke in opposite directions.

Konantz continued his pursuit of the leader, who took violent evasive action no more than fifty feet above the ground. Coming upon a brewery, with its high brick chimney, the German endeavoured to throw off his adversary by pulling about 4g in a tight turn around the smokestack! Holding him, Konantz got in a burst of fire which took out part of the Me 109's left aileron, causing the fighter to snap to an inverted position. The pilot skilfully righted his aircraft before descending over the snow-covered countryside. Konantz registered more hits, and the Me 109 bellied-in and slid over half a mile into some trees. As Konantz flew over the wreckage he saw the pilot emerge and raise an arm in salute. Both the other Me 109s met their end in a similar fashion.

Near a half century later, in a letter to an aviation magazine, artist Brooks Whelan solicited background material for a series of action paintings he planned. One of those responding was Konantz, now a retired USAF major, who provided information on combats in which he was involved, including his recent discovery of the identity of the Me 109 pilot he had brought down on 29 January 1945. To Konantz's surprise, one of the historians who assisted in the German pilot's identification also put him in touch with Horst Petzschler, then living in Wichita, Kansas, who had been in the same unit as the three Me 109s. The previous day he had been leading a flight of former bomber pilots from a Silesian airfield to a training base in Denmark. All except Petzschler were officers who used their rank to divert to Hamburg to spend the night with relations. Horst flew on to Denmark alone. The three Me 109 pilots took off from Hamburg, only to be intercepted by the Mustangs. Konantz learned in 1992 that the leading Me 109G he had brought down was piloted by Oberleutnant Waldemar Balasus, who survived hostilities and died in 1989.

Brooks Whelan has captured the tight pursuit round the brewery chimney with *Saturday Night*, Konantz's P-51D, blasting Balasus' 'Blue 32'. Whelan had more than a feel for the German terrain and situation, for on the date of the encounter he was a US Army radio operator with a British armoured unit close to the front line in north-west Europe.

'Los Angeles City Limits'

DOUGLAS ETTRIDGE

SHAFTS of winter sunlight penetrate the clouds as Fortress *Los Angeles City Limits* makes a landing approach to an RAF airfield, one of the pre-war type hangars being visible in this atmospheric painting. Children on a public road and the farmer's wife feeding her hens look up as the giant passes low overhead, its four Wright Cyclones throttled back and its flaps partly lowered. Snow carpets the English countryside and the air has the bite of frost on this January afternoon in 1945.

Named in honour of America's West Coast metropolis, *Los Angeles City Limits*—officially B-17G 42-107018—was delivered to the 535th Bomb Squadron at Ridgewell, Essex, in March 1944, one of the first Fortresses received at that station in unpainted finish. Its combat initiation was to Cotbus on 11 April, and by October it had completed 60 missions without ever having to turn back because of mechanical problems. On its 61st sortie it had a rare encounter with an Me 163 rocket-propelled fighter, but despite battle damage was able to return to home base.

By May 1945 this bomber had completed over a hundred sorties in the hands of two dozen different crews during thirteen months of combat operations. Like most of the Eighth Air Force B-17s that were flown back to the United States in the summer of 1945 it ended its days in the vast salvage park at Kingman, Arizona.

The painting, as with more than a hundred others from Douglas Ettridge's brush, is in the private gallery of Mr and Mrs Dee Howard of Texas. Much of the artist's work is held by US collectors, and, although currently resident in the United Kingdom, Douglas Ettridge regularly visits America and lived there for a number of years.

'Guardian Angels'

JIM LAURIER

A 'FINGER four' of P-51D Mustangs flying escort for a group of B-17 Fortresses provides the subject for this oil on canvas. The black and white chequerboard with red trim was the hallmark of the 78th Fighter Group and the leading Mustang, *Big Beautiful Doll*, is that of the Commanding Officer, Colonel John D. Landers.

In a year of flying with the Eighth Air Force, Landers served with three different fighter groups and was officially credited with $8^1/_2$ aerial victories and with destroying another twenty aircraft on enemy airfields. Before coming to England he flew combat in the south-west Pacific area of operations and shot down six Japanese aircraft. A static P-51D exhibited by the Imperial War Museum in England is painted to represent *Big Beautiful Doll*.

The Mustang positioned as wingman to Landers on the right of the flight, tail number 463632 and carrying the nickname *Lee D*, was the aircraft usually flown by 1st Lieutenant William DeGain.

Below the 'silver' Mustangs are Fortresses carrying the markings of the 303rd Bomb Group. Dubbed the 'Hell's Angels Group', the 303rd was one of the four pioneer B-17 groups of the Eighth Air Force that developed operational procedure during the winter of 1942–43.

'Rough Deal'

HARRY CLOW

A DRAMATIC moment at Hardwick airfield as a battered Liberator comes in to land. No 3 engine has a feathered propeller while No 2 has taken fire which is spreading rapidly. A shell hole in the right wing and a lacerated rudder are further evidence of enemy action which has given the B-24's crew a rough deal. The pursuing Dodge ambulance and a rescue truck will probably be needed in what looks like an impending crash-landing. The time is the very hard winter of 1944–45 when snow persisted for several weeks in January. The late afternoon sky has signs that it may clear and give another frosty night.

The subject Liberator is a B-24J of the 329th Bomb Squadron, a unit specialising in the use of G-H radar pathfinding, its aircraft frequently leading the formations of other bomb groups. G-H was a British development consisting of a transmitter/receiver in the aircraft interrogating two beacons in England constantly to fix its position. G-H was extremely accurate, enabling effective 'blind' attacks on cloud-obscured targets up to a range of 300 miles. The 329th's Liberators were identified by red-painted noses, as that in Harry Clow's painting.

The squadron was one of four that composed the 93rd Bomb Group, which was the first organisation in the Eighth Air Force to enter combat with the Liberator. Between October 1942 and May 1945 the group participated in 396 combat missions, a total greater than that of any other Eighth Air Force bomb group, although 49 of these were flown from bases in North Africa. Losses amounted to 1,150 men killed, wounded and taken prisoner from 100 B-24s lost on operations and another 40 destroyed in accidents.

'The Judas Goat'

JOHN RABBETS

THE most colourfully bizarre aircraft flying in the United Kingdom during the Second World War were without question the 8th Air Force bombers used for leading group formation assemblies. During the winter of 1943–44 the 2nd Bomb Division, in particular, witnessed a number of occasions when bombers from one unit inadvertently joined the formation of another during the pre-mission activity in the crowded airspace over East Anglia. This was most notable when formations gathered in darkness or poor weather. One solution to the problem was to take a war-weary B-24 and give it a distinctive paint scheme, install electric lights in the form of the group identity symbol in the fuselage sides, and use the aircraft specifically as a marker on which combat B-24s of the group could form. Known by a number of different terms but chiefly as an Assembly Ship, this aircraft also carried a large supply of pyrotechnics used by crew members continually to fire identification colours from the waist windows.

In operation, the Assembly Ship would take off first, climb and orbit in the group's assembly area with illuminations switched on and discharging flares. When the formation was established the Assembly Ship would return to home base while the formation it had aided joined the divisional column and went to war. This procedure led to another epithet, 'Judas Goat', after the biblical animal that led others to slaughter.

The painting, originally commissioned for the jacket of *Mighty Eighth War Diary* in 1980, depicts the 453rd Bomb Group's yellow-chequered *Wham Bam* with Liberators of the 735th Bomb Squadron. *Wham Bam* was an original combat B-24D of the 330th Bomb Squadron, 93rd Bomb Group, that came to England in the autumn of 1942. In February 1944 the veteran was transferred for use as an Assembly Ship at Old Buckenham and remained in service with the 453rd Group until declared salvage in May 1945.

Until his retirement to Yorkshire, artist John Rabbets, well known for his coloured aircraft profiles in *The Mighty Eighth*, was the head of a college art department.

'Ronnie Returns'

JOHN CONSTABLE REEVE

INDIVIDUAL aircraft became well known and even famous in the units that operated them either through their extraordinary endurance or because of the incidents in which they were involved. Pride of the 446th Bomb Group at Bungay airfield was a Liberator called *Ronnie*. The B-24H was so named in honour of a waist-gunner of the original assigned crew, S/Sgt Ronald Gannon, who was struck down by a wasting disease while the Group was training near Denver, Colorado, and died.

Ronnie came to England with the 446th and, after a troubled start with engineering problems, in the capable hands of crew chief M/Sgt Michael Zyne the bomber began to amass a higher total of missions completed than any other Liberator in the Group. After 79 without a turnback for mechanical failure, the nosewheel collapsed when the aircraft was setting out for the next mission, damaging the nose. A new nose was grafted to the fuselage and after a few weeks *Ronnie* was once again in service.

On 30 December 1944 this Liberator flew its hundredth mission, but six days later, on what would have been its 102nd, severe mechanical difficulties forced a landing on an airstrip in liberated France. The 446th was determined to retrieve the veteran and in March it was back at Bungay flying missions. On 10 April 1945 *Ronnie* was in a 446th Bomb Group formation dropping fragmentation bombs on the Luftwaffe airfield at Rechlin. Two bombs from an aircraft higher in the formation apparently collided in their fall and exploded, peppering *Ronnie*. The pilot flew the bomber back to Manston, where three of the crew elected to bale out. However, a successful landing was made despite two flat tyres and damaged tail controls. Once more *Ronnie* was resurrected but hostilities were concluded. The 119-mission veteran was still in sound enough condition for the 446th Group Commanding Officer to fly the bomber across the Atlantic back to the United States. It was eventually flown down to a storage site in New Mexico, there to await the breakers.

The painting depicts *Ronnie* about to touch down at Bungay. Other B-24s can be seen on the far side of the airfield on their dispersal points, near one of the black T2 model hangars.

'Wolfpack Leader Downs Five'

JERRY CRANDALL

A BEAUTIFUL rendering of the personal Republic Thunderbolt of Colonel David Schilling which he flew while commanding the 56th Fighter Group during the last quarter of 1944. Carrying a 'Hairless Joe' motif, a character from the popular newspaper comic strip Lil' Abner, this was the first P-47D-25 received by the 62nd Fighter Squadron, and it was used by Dave Schilling to achieve several of his 22^1/$_2$ air victories. The D-25 model Thunderbolt introduced the so-called 'bubble' canopy over the cockpit, giving better visibility for the pilot.

On 23 December 1944, during the last main German ground offensive in the West, the 56th Fighter Group was vectored by a radar controller to large concentrations of enemy fighters which the Luftwaffe had put up in an effort to counter Allied air activity. There was considerable haze and cirrus cloud at high altitude, and the 56th, flying at 26,000 feet, was unable to close on the enemy reported in the first two vectors. A third direction from the radar controller was

successful and the Thunderbolts were able to carry out a surprise attack from the rear on formations composed of an estimated hundred Me 109s and FW 190s. Having the advantage, the Thunderbolt pilots shot down 37 of the enemy for the loss of only three of their number. Colonel Schilling himself was credited with five victories during the extensive air battle that raged in the Bonn area for several minutes.

Dave Schilling was also credited with a total of 10 aircraft destroyed on enemy airfields by strafing during his two combat tours. An extremely popular personality, he continued an Air Force career after the war, but he was killed in a car accident in England in 1956.

In addition to being an accomplished artist, Jerry Crandall is an expert on the American West and has been involved in a number of television productions covering this subject. His aircraft paintings stem principally from his enthusiasm for Second World War aviation and his collection of related photographs, artefacts and memorabilia.

'Thundering Home'

NICOLAS TRUDGIAN

IN an evening setting, a loose formation of B-17 Fortresses is joined by two B-24 Liberators and a pair of P-51 Mustangs as the participants of a raid on the Reich head home over the North Sea to their bases in East Anglia. Other Liberators can be seen in the distance of this colourful composition. Such cloudscapes, a familiar sight to the aircrews, were a frequent obstacle to the execution of a bombing mission.

This Nicolas Trudgian canvas typifies the might of the Eighth Air Force in the closing months of hostilities. The central image, Fortress number 483484, a late model B-17G assigned to the 94th Bomb Group in the spring of 1945, has the red-painted engine cowlings that distinguished the 332nd Bomb Squadron at that time. This and the other B-17s in the formation have yellow empennages and wing tips,

the identifying markings of the 4th Combat Bomb Wing, a tactical organisation of which the 94th Bomb Group was part. Their Wing Headquarters shared the Bury St Edmunds base with this group. One of the three original groups of the 3rd Division, which controlled all the B-17 bases in the county of Suffolk, the 94th was in combat for two years, flying 324 missions and having 153 of its bombers missing in action.

The two B-24s in the painting display the red tail with white vertical stripe of the 458th Bomb Group based at Horsham St Faith, an airfield that eventually became Norwich Airport. Red and white chequerboard noses identify the Mustangs of the 339th Fighter Group which operated from Fowlmere, south of Cambridge.

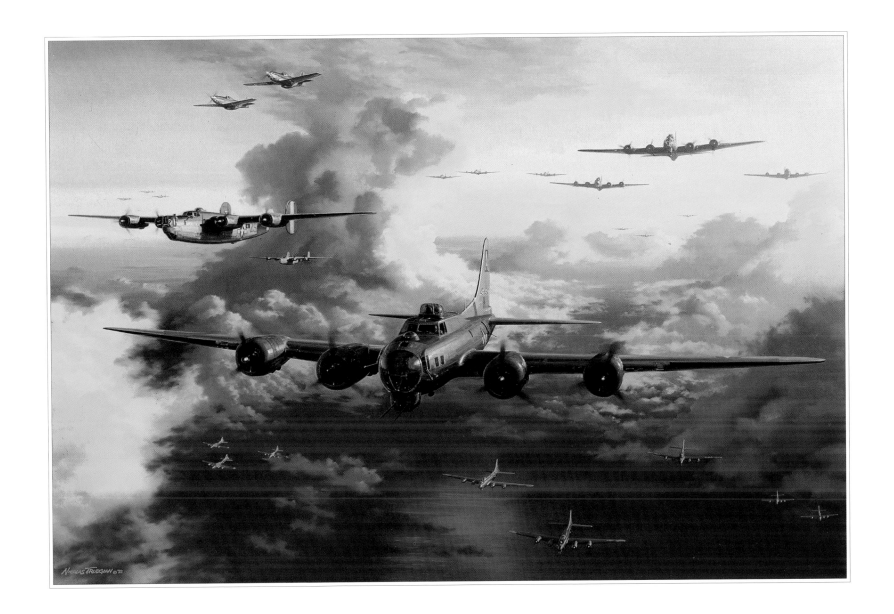

'A Bluestocking For Camilla'

GERALD ASHER

THE De Havilland Mosquito Mk XVI, with its high speed, long range, two-man crew and good equipment stowage capacity, was sought by the Eighth Air Force for multi-purpose reconnaissance and combat mission support roles. The first examples, obtained from the RAF in the early spring of 1944, equipped two squadrons at Watton, Norfolk.

The 653rd Bombardment Squadron (Reconnaissance, Special) had as its primary mission the gathering of weather information over or near enemy territory. This took two forms, 'Scout' sorties which preceded heavy bomber missions to determine the weather conditions and to report the observations by radio to task force leaders, and 'Bluestocking' sorties to obtain meteorological information from specific areas over or near enemy territory for the purposes of weather forecasting. Most Scout missions were taken over by special Mustang units later in 1944 and the majority of 653rd Bomb Squadron operations comprised 1,131 Bluestocking flights, more than 900 of them in hostile airspace.

One of the Mosquitos received during May 1944, direct from production, serialled NS569 and given the nickname *Camilla*, participated in several Scout and Bluestocking sorties during the spring and summer of 1944. Following the provisional organisation at Watton

becoming the 25th Bomb Group (Rcn. Sp.) in August 1944, *Camilla* flew only one further Bluestocking before being damaged and scrapped in April 1945. This sortie was on 8 February 1945 when the aircraft took off from Watton at 0142 hours to cover south-east Germany, returning at 0533 hours. The pilot was Captain Larkin and the navigator Captain John Walsh. The latter, the Group Navigator, lost his life in a clandestine mission in April 1945 when the aircraft in which he was flying hit a balloon cable on the Netherlands coast at night.

Camilla is featured in Gerald Asher's painting as she appeared on her last Bluestocking. The darker blue discs on fuselage and wings are where the British roundels were painted over, contrasting with the faded 'PR Blue' of the original paintwork. The all-red empennage was a feature of the day-flying Mosquitos of the 25th Group from the autumn of 1944 to identify the type as friendly. This red painting was applied after two incidents where these lone reconnaissance aircraft had been attacked by Allied fighters. The letter 'N' on the fin is *Camilla*'s radio call-sign and the circular blue background distinguishes the 653rd from the other Mosquito-equipped squadron of the 25th Group.

'Retirement Party for Old Thunder Bird'

KEITH FERRIS

IN 1966 Keith Ferris was introduced to his next door neighbour's brother, Fred Stewart, who had flown B-17s with the Eighth Air Force in England. An enthusiast for the type, Fred produced a miniature B-17 pilot's checklist from his wallet together with a number of photographs of service with the 303rd Bomb Group. One picture was of the bomber in which he had flown his first combat mission on 22 March 1945, a worn, camouflaged B-17G named *Thunder Bird*. The mission also proved to be the bomber's last for, on return, engineering officers declared it too weary to be used for further operations.

Thunder Bird, originally assigned to the 359th Bomb Squadron, had been received at the 303rd Group's Molesworth base in January 1944. During the following fourteen months it completed 116 missions, not without collecting several perforations from flak. Following its retirement from combat it was passed to another group and flown back to the United States at the end of hostilities, eventually meeting its end in the huge breakers' yard at Kingman, Arizona. Keith Ferris decided to feature this aircraft in a painting he planned and his result shows *Thunder Bird* ploughing through a flak barrage, with No 3 propeller feathered, while on its final mission.

Thunder Bird as portrayed on this Fortress was a mythical bird, the sight of which could bring distress and havoc to those who perceived its form. It was the name that certain North American Indians gave to aeroplanes from their first sight and sound of a flying machine. This impressive painting led, ten years later, to a commission from the National Air and Space Museum in Washington, DC, for a mural featuring the same aircraft. 'Fortresses under Fire' covers the entire back wall of the World War II Gallery, being 25 feet high and 75 feet wide, and depicts *Thunder Bird* and other B-17s of the 303rd Bomb Group as on the mission of 15 August 1944 to a target at Wiesbaden. Although reproductions of this mural are prohibited through the agreement of artist and NASM not to commercialise the work, it has become what is probably the most famous of all paintings featuring Eighth Air Force subjects.

Keith Ferris is one of the world's premier aviation artists and his work is to be found in many prestigious locations in the United States, including the US Air Force Academy at Colorado Springs and the USAF Museum at Dayton, Ohio.

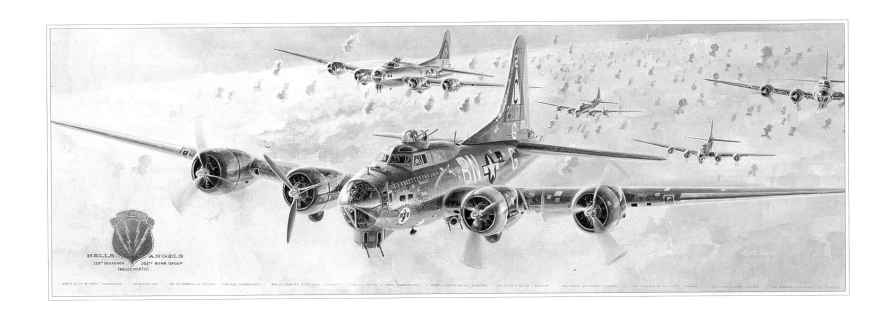

'Scat VII'

DAVID POOLE

Of all American Second World War combat aircraft, more P-51 Mustangs survive a half century on than any other type. Surprisingly, several of these are machines that were actually used in combat during the closing stages of hostilities. David Poole's evocation of Major Robin Olds shooting down an FW 190 features the latter's personal P-51D, serial number 44-72922 and named *Scat VII*, which survives in private ownership still in an airworthy condition.

Following VE-Day many Mustangs with low flying hours were transferred from operational units to Speke airfield, Liverpool, where they were partly dismantled and shipped back to the United States. Some were then re-issued to active flying units, but 44-72922 went into storage for several years until the USAF no longer had use for P-51s and they were disposed of on the commercial market. In February 1958 this aircraft was sold for $1,196 at McClellan Air Force Base, California, to Robert H. Fee. Modified and used as a civilian runaround, over the next thirty years it passed through nine owners. In the late 1980s the historic significance of the airframe came to be appreciated and in 1992 the current owner, Jim Shuttleworth of Huntington, Indiana, set about returning the aircraft to its wartime configuration and markings.

Robin Olds is the son of General Robert C. Olds, a stalwart of the pre-war US Army Air Corps and commander of the first group to receive the B-17. Young Robin can be said to have had flying in his blood and as a 19-year-old 2nd Lieutenant he was sent to England as a member of the P-38-equipped 479th Fighter Group, the last fighter unit to join the Eighth Air Force. He soon proved to be one of the ablest pilots in the group and within a year he had the rank of Major and command of the 434th Fighter Squadron. His score of air victories stood at 12 , one of the highest in the group, and he also destroyed another ten enemy aircraft by ground strafing. In later years Robin Olds commanded an F-4 Phantom organisation in the Vietnam conflict, being credited with another four air victories. His personal aircraft were still nicknamed *Scat*.

The original David Poole art of *Scat VII* shooting down an FW 190 on 19 March 1945 is in the Dimitri Rotow collection and is reproduced here with his permission.

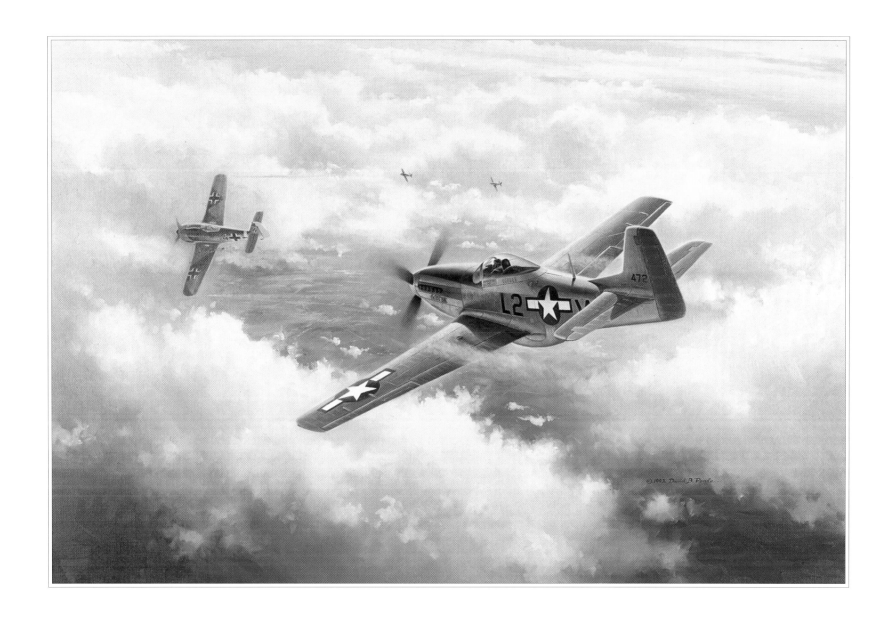

'Major Alva Murphy'

MERLE OLMSTED

MAJOR Alva C. Murphy, credited with six aerial victories while flying with the 357th Fighter Group, obtained these as 'doubles' in three actions; the last of these took place on 2 March 1945. Then, having shot down two of the enemy Me 109s in a dogfight, Murphy's Mustang was hit by flak while strafing an airfield. With his engine losing coolant he baled out and was seen to land safely in a field. However, Luftwaffe documents show his body recovered and buried. Despite the US authorities' extensive efforts in the immediate post-war years to establish the fate of missing and dead airmen, no other information has come to light on what happened to Alva Murphy.

As the Third Reich moved towards inevitable defeat, there were many instances of Allied pilots being killed by hostile German civilians. Wehrmacht personnel usually honoured the Geneva Convention on the treatment of prisoners but many civilians, particularly those who had been subjected to or had witnessed strafing attacks by fighters, had few qualms about lynching captives before they were taken by the military.

Artist Merle Olmsted, serving as a 19-year-old Assistant Crew Chief in Murphy's original unit, the 362nd Fighter Squadron, knew the 22 year-old pilot. His appreciation of this capable fighter ace shows Murphy stepping into the cockpit of a P-51D. He wears typical fighter pilot garb of the time: a Mutton-collar B-4 flying jacket over coveralls and a yellow Mae West inflatable lifejacket under his parachute harness. The oxygen mask hangs from one side of the A-11 flying helmet on which a pair of RAF Mk VIII goggles rest.

Merle Olmsted used his talents with a paintbrush during his time with the 362nd Fighter Squadron, applying some of the nicknames as requested by pilots. In later years he would become the 357th Group's historian, publishing two books on its war record. His art is primarily devoted to subjects relating to his days at Leiston.

'Upupa epops and Friends'

NOEL DUNN

NOEL Dunn's art covers such diverse subjects as hunting and fishing, birds, dogs, cowboys, landscapes and aviation. An enthusiast for flight, he served in the US Air Force and Minnesota Air National Guard from 1961 to 1967. Since then he has pursued his particular interest in individual Second World War aircraft associated with notable veterans of that conflict. He has amassed nearly a hundred paintings in this historic collection, all signed by men who flew, or were associated with, the aircraft.

The trio of Mustangs of the 352nd Fighter Squadron, 353rd Fighter Group, features aircraft 472364, which was received by Captain Harrison Tordoff on 1 March 1945 and flown by him to the war's end. The name he chose for the fighter, *Upupa epops*, is the scientific name of the hoopoe, 'a bizarre European bird of untidy habits and unsteady flight'. Flying *Upupa epops*, Bud Tordoff shot down an Me 262 jet on 31 March 1945 and an Me 109 on 7 April, which gave him the five victories that constituted the unofficial accolade of 'ace'. His earlier successes were gained during a first operational tour with the 353rd the previous year. Some forty years later Bud Tordoff was greatly surprised to learn the *Upupa epops* was still in existence and had not gone to the breakers, the fate of most warplanes in the immediate years after the end of the Second World War.

Having very low flying hours, the P-51D had been retained by the USAAF and served with units in Germany for two years. It was then purchased by the Swedes, who sold it on to the Dominican Air Force in 1952. The aircraft remained with that service for 32 years until acquired, together with five other Mustangs, by Brian O'Farrell of Johnson Aviation in Florida. It is now being restored to flying condition and repainted in its wartime markings, and it will be used as a personal display aircraft.

The other P-51s carrying the 353rd Fighter Group's eye-catching black and yellow chequerboard in Noel Dunn's painting are Captain Don Barber's *Gloria Ann 2nd* and *Double Trouble Two*, the latter being the personal mount of Lieutenant-Colonel William Bailey, a 353rd Headquarters officer.

'The Last Mission'

BRYAN MOON

FORTRESSES of the 91st Bomb Group, 'The Ragged Irregulars', resplendent in bare metal finish and the red identification markings of the 1st Combat Wing, set against a cloudscape while returning from the Group's 338th mission.

The significance of this mission for the radio operator in the nearest aircraft was that it was the thirtieth and last of his combat tour. TSgt Merrel L. Duncan was a lead crew radio operator for the 91st Group, selected because of his expertise in this vital and responsible post. The Fortress in which he flew on 18 April 1945 to bomb the marshalling yards at Rosenheim was named *Tennessee Tess,* a B-17G specially equipped as a visual leadplane and on this occasion piloted by Captain R. R. Goldsmith. *Tennessee Tess* was assigned to the 91st Group's 401st Bomb Squadron early in November 1944 and served as the Group's leader on several missions up to the end of hostilities.

The accompanying B-17 in the picture, marked 'LL:E', was named *The Peacemaker.* Delivered to the 401st Bomb Squadron in June 1944, it was frequently shot up by flak and fighters, only to be destroyed in a flying accident in England during April 1945. Bryan Moon's pastel was commissioned by Merrel Duncan's son and marketed in a limited print run with copies of the radio operator's personal diary of his combat experiences.

The artist was born in the United Kingdom and emigrated to the United States in 1966. Having held various offices in both the British and American aviation industries, he took early retirement as a Vice-President of Northwest Airlines in 1987 to pursue his love of art. His interest covers a wide range of topics, usually with a historical significance. Bryan Moon's aviation prints are unusual in that they are mostly marketed with an artefact connected with the subject.

The Artists

Contributors' addresses and telephone numbers for use in commissioning work or acquiring prints. Current January 1996.

Gerald Asher, Fox 3 Studios, 6837 Northpark Drive, Fort Worth, Texas 76180, USA. Tel: (817) 581-0304.

Mike Bailey, 91 Waterworks Road, Norwich, Norfolk NR2 4DB, England. Tel: 01603-626257.

Robert Bailey, 4 Brightbank Avenue, Stony Plain, Alberta T7Z 1G6, Canada. Tel: (403) 963-5480.

Mel Brown, 8415 Red Willow, Austin, Texas 78736, USA. Tel: (512) 288-7354.

Derek Bunce, 36 Clarence Road, Walton-on-Thames, Surrey, KT12 5JY, England.

Gil Cohen, 62 Creek Drive, Doylestown, Pennsylvania 18901-4717, USA. Tel: (215) 348-0779.

Harry Clow, Broadacres, Cookes Road, Thurton, Norfolk NR14 6AE, England. Tel: 01508-480302.

Jerry Crandall, PO Box 2606, Sedona, Arizona 86336, USA. Tel: (602) 284-1068.

Noel Dunn, 767 East Roselawn Avenue, Maplewood, Minnesota 55117, USA. Tel: (612) 772-1603.

Douglas Ettridge, Quiet Waters, Roundstone Lane, Angmering, Sussex BN16 4AX, England. Tel: 01903-773686

Keith Ferris, Keith Ferris, Inc., 50 Moraine Road, Morris Plains, New Jersey 07950, USA. Tel: (201) 539-3363.

Chris French, 25 Romney Close, Braintree, Essex CM7 5TE, England. Tel: 01376-328562.

Nixon Galloway, Studio G Inc., 755 Marine Avenue, Manhattan Beach, California 90266, USA. Tel: (310) 545-7709.

Howard Gerrard, Layve Oast, Snughorne Lane, Smarden, Kent TN27 8PR, England. Tel: 01233-770671.

Roy Grinnell, 2550 East Avenida De Maria, Tucson, Arizona 85718, USA. Tel: (520) 577-8825.

Keith Hill, 24 St.Peter's Avenue, Rushden, Northamptonshire NN10 6XW, England. Tel: 01933-50283.

Peter Hurd. c/o US Army Center of Military History, 1099 14th Street NW., Washington, DC 20005-3402, USA.

Jim Laurier, PO Box 1118, Keene, New Hampshire 03431, USA. Tel: (603) 357-2051.

Bryan Moon, Moon Studios, RR2, 29402 Lake Avenue, Frontenac, Minnesota 55026, USA. Tel: (612) 345-4437.

Merle Olmsted, 6803 Rexdale Lane, Paradise, California 95969, USA. Tel: (916) 877-3960

Jack Olson, c/o Seattle Museum of Flight, 9404 East Marginal Way South, Seattle, Washington 98101, USA. Tel (206) 764-5707

Geoff Pleasance, 195 Henniker Road, Ipswich, Suffolk IP1 5HH, England. Tel: 01473-747673.

David Poole, P.O. Box 12983, Roanoke, Virginia 24030, USA. Tel: (703) 977-2017.

John Rabbets, Shude Rise, Goodmanham, Market Weighton, York YO4 3HX, England. Tel: 01430-873137

John Constable Reeve, Prospect Farm, Mettingham, Bungay, Suffolk NR35 1TS, England. Tel: 01986-892696.

Stan Stokes, P.O. Box 1420, Pebble Beach, California 93953, USA. Tel: (408) 625-5017.

Robert Taylor, The Military Gallery, 1 & 2 Queens Parade Place, Bath BA1 1NN, England. Tel: 01225-427521.

Nicolas Trudgian, The Military Gallery, 1 & 2 Queens Parade Place, Bath BA1 1NN, Avon, England. Tel: 01225-427521.

Matthew Waki, 353 Scott Avenue, Salt Lake City, Utah 84115-4618, USA. Tel: (801) 484-1980.

Brooks Whelan, Art Service, Box 512, South Orleans, Massachusetts 02662, USA. Tel: (800) 866-3442.

Ronald Wong, 15 Henderson Close, St. Albans, Hertfordshire AL3 6DY, England. Tel: 01727-869917.

Frank Wootton OBE, Mayflower House, Alfriston, Sussex BN26 5QT, England. Tel: 01323-870343.

John Young, Sherewood House, 186 White Hill, Chesham, Buckinghamshire HP51AZ, England. Tel: 01494-782589.